Fall in Love with You

Walter Riso

EMBRACE YOUR AUTHENTICITY THROUGH
THE ESSENTIAL VALUE OF SELF-ESTEEM

Fall in Love with You

Planeta Books

Original title: *Enamórate de ti: El valor imprescindible de la autoestima*

© 1990, Walter Riso
c/o Schavelzon Graham Agencia Literaria
www.schavelzongraham.com

Translation: © 2024, Azzam Alkadhi

Cover design: © Genoveva Saavedra / aciditadiseño
Cover illustration: © iStock.com/hofred
Author photo: © Antonio Navarro Wijmark
Interior design: © Juan Carlos González Juárez

All rights reserved.

© 2025, Editorial Planeta Mexicana, S.A. de C.V.
Under the imprint PLANETABOOKS
Avenida Presidente Masarik 111, Piso 2, Polanco V Sección,
Miguel Hidalgo, Ciudad de México, MEX 11560
www.planetadelibros.us

First edition in this format: August 2025
ISBN: 978-607-39-1992-0

Total or partial reproduction of this book or its incorporation into a computer system or transmitted in any form or by any means is not permitted, whether electronic, mechanical, photocopying, recording or otherwise, without the prior written permission from the *copyright* holders.

The use or reproduction of this book or any part of it for the purpose of training or feeding Artificial Intelligence (AI) systems or technologies is expressly prohibited.

The violation of these rights may constitute an offense against intellectual property. (Arts. 229 and following of the Ley Federal del Derecho de Autor and Arts. 424 and following of the Código Penal Federal.)

If you need a photocopy or scanning of any part of this work, please refer to CeMPro. (Centro Mexicano de Protección y Fomento de los Derechos de Autor, http://www.cempro.org.mx.)

Printed by Bertelsmann Printing Group USA
25 Jack Enders Boulevard, Berryville, Virginia 22611, USA.
Printed in the United States of America

*For my parents,
Fernando and Dora*

At one pole of my being, I am one with sticks and stones. There I have to acknowledge the rule of universal law. That is where the foundation of my existence lies, deep down below. Its strength lies in its being held firm in the clasp of the comprehensive world, and in the fullness of its community with all things.

But at the other pole of my being, I am separate from all. There I have broken through the cordon of equality and stand alone as an individual. I am absolutely unique, I am I, I am incomparable. The whole weight of the universe cannot crush out this individuality of mine. I maintain it in spite of the tremendous gravitation of all things. It is small in appearance but great in reality. For it holds its own against the forces that would rob it of its distinction and make it one with the dust.

—Rabindranath Tagore

CONTENTS

INTRODUCTION xiii

CHAPTER 1: **FALL IN LOVE WITH YOU**. 1
   The Four Pillars of Self-Esteem 4

CHAPTER 2: **DEVELOP A GOOD SELF-CONCEPT** 9
   Bad Self-Criticism 10
   Self-Labeling: "I am" or "I behaved"? 14
   Ruthless Demands of Yourself 14
   All or Nothing 17
   Change and Revision 18
   Saving Your Self-Concept 20
      1. *Try to Be More Flexible with Yourself*
         and Others 20
      2. *Review Your Goals and the Realistic*
         Chance of Reaching Them 23
      3. *Don't Just See the Bad in Yourself* 24
      4. *Don't Think Poorly of Yourself* 24

    5. *Love Yourself for as Much Time as Possible* **25**
    6. *Try to Move Your "Ideal Me" Closer to Your "Real Me"* **26**
    7. *Learn to Lose* **27**

CHAPTER 3: DEVELOP A GOOD SELF-IMAGE **29**
The Weight of Comparison **30**
The Personal Magnifying Glass **32**
Mirror, Mirror… **33**
Inventing Beauty **34**
Improving Your Self-Image **38**
    1. *Try to Define Your Own Beauty or Aesthetic Criteria* **38**
    2. *Discard Physical Perfection and Strict Criteria* **38**
    3. *Discover and Highlight the Things You Like about Yourself* **39**
    4. *Your Self-Image Is Communicated to Others* **40**
    5. *Physical Appearance Is Only One Part of Self-Image* **41**
    6. *Don't Magnify What You Don't Like about Yourself* **42**
    7. *There Will Always Be Someone Willing to Love You* **43**
    8. *Don't Make Unfair Comparisons* **44**

Chapter 4: Develop Good Self-Reinforcement 47
Hedonistic Philosophy 50
   Explorative Behavior 52
   The Ability to Feel: "I feel, therefore I am" 53
   A Case of Emotional Restriction of Joy 59
Self-Praise 61
   Three Irrational Beliefs that Stop Us From Congratulating Ourselves 62
   External Praise that Can Become Self-Praise 64
   How to Praise Yourself 67
   A Self-Praise Summary 69
Treating and Rewarding Yourself 70
   The Culture of Miserliness, or When Saving Becomes a Problem 73
   You Are Not the Exception: You Need to Reward Yourself 75
   Stop Worshipping Repression 77
Improving Your Self-Reinforcement 82
   1. Make Time for Pleasure 82
   2. Decide to Live Hedonistically 83
   3. Don't Rationalize Pleasant Emotions So Much 84
   4. Activate Self-Praise and Put It to Work 87
   5. Be Modest, But Don't Overdo It 88
   6. Treat Yourself 89
   7. Fight Against Psychological and Emotional Repression 90

CHAPTER 5: **DEVELOP STRONG SELF-EFFICACY** 93
   Three Causes of Weak Self-Efficacy 95
      The Perception that Nothing Can Be Done . . 97
      The Internal Locus of Control 99
      Attributional Styles 102
   The Avoidance Problem 104
      Is the Danger Real? 107
   Overcoming Weak Self-Efficacy 109
     1. Eliminate "I'm not capable" from Your Vocabulary 110
     2. Don't Be a Pessimist 111
     3. Don't Be Fatalistic 113
     4. Try to Be a Realist 115
     5. Don't Only Remember the Bad Things . . . 116
     6. Review Your Goals 117
     7. Test Yourself and Take a Risk 118

EPILOGUE 121

BIBLIOGRAPHY 125

INTRODUCTION

Loving yourself is the best form of defense against mental suffering. It is not only a yardstick for measuring how much we should love others (i.e., "Love thy neighbor as thyself"), but it also appears to provide protection from psychological illnesses and is key to generating well-being and quality of life.

Activating all your available self-esteem or loving your essence is the first step toward any kind of psychological growth and personal development. And I'm not referring to the dark side: arrogance, narcissism, and an obsession with the ego and feeling unique, special, and better than others; nor am I talking about a blind, insatiable crush on the "I" (egocentricity). I am referring to the genuine capacity to recognize, without fear or shame, the strengths and virtues we possess, to integrate them in our daily lives, and shower others with them effectively and compassionately. Loving yourself while looking down on or ignoring others is presumptuous and exclusive; loving others while you look down on yourself is a lack of self-love.

"Fall in love with you" means "Love yourself sincerely," persist in your own being (*conatus*), as Spinoza explained, in order to defend individual existence and bring out the best in each of us. Loving yourself is also fostering healthy self-preservation, as promoted by the Stoics, and seeking maximum pleasure and health, as pursued by Epicurus. Loving yourself is considering yourself to be worthy of the best; it is bolstering self-respect and giving yourself the opportunity to be happy for the sole reason that you are alive.

Love starts at home. Your first love story is the one you have with yourself; in this first romance you will learn to love or hate existence. How can you open the doors of love to those around you if you belittle yourself or fail to accept your being, or if you are ashamed to exist? A patient crushed by depression used to say to me, "I'm sorry, but… I'm ashamed to be alive." Could there be any greater form of decay? Just as you do not attack or shun those you love, don't do it to yourself. Being your own friend is the first step toward having self-esteem. Love is looking for the best in others and enjoying it, and the same applies to self-love: If you don't forgive yourself, if being with yourself annoys you, if you can't bear yourself, and if you put yourself down, you don't love yourself! Sometimes I get asked if it is possible to hate yourself, and my answer is unequivocal, "Of course, and with tremendous intensity!" Up to the point of wanting to fall off the face of the earth and acting accordingly to make that happen.

We often take pleasure in self-inflicted pain. There's a story about a woman on a train at three in the morning; while everyone else was asleep, she started complaining loudly, "My God, I'm so thirsty! My God, I'm so thirsty," over and over again. Her persistence woke the other passengers and the man beside her went and brought her two glasses of water, saying, "Here you go, quench your thirst so that we can all go to sleep." The woman quickly drank them, and everyone got comfortable again. Everything seemed to return to normal until, a few minutes later, the woman was heard saying, "My God, I *was* so thirsty! My God, I *was* so thirsty!" We incorporate psychological punishment into our lives from an early age without realizing it, and we adapt to it as if it were a normal facet—and even desirable. We delight in suffering or put it on a pedestal. At times we act as if self-punishment were a virtue because it "hardens the soul"; and while it is important to strive to achieve our personal goals, constructive self-criticism is not the same as the savage self-criticism that batters and buries us. It is one thing to accept useful and necessary suffering, and quite another to get used to the pain we masochistically inflict on ourselves to "cleanse us of guilt" or "try to be worthy" of someone loving us.

Findings from the cognitive psychology field over the last twenty years clearly show that the negative view we hold of ourselves is a determining factor in the onset of psychological disorders such as phobias, depression, stress, anxiety, interpersonal insecurity, psychosomatic conditions, relationship problems, underperformance at school and work, substance abuse, body image disorders, inability to regulate emotions, and much more. The conclusion from specialists is clear: If our self-esteem is not sufficiently high, we will live poorly, we will be unhappy, and we will suffer from anxiety.

This book is for people who don't love themselves enough, who live isolated lives, cling to irrational rules, and are inconsiderate to themselves. It is also for those who once knew how to love themselves, but have forgotten in the intensity of daily life or the frenzied race for survival, which makes us put ourselves on the back burner, as if we were disposable. The aim of this book is both simple and complex: to show you how to fall in love with yourself; how to be brave; how to start a supportive relationship with yourself that will make you increasingly happy and resilient to daily struggles.

CHAPTER 1

FALL IN LOVE WITH YOU

Loving ourselves is perhaps the most important factor in guaranteeing our survival in a complex world that is increasingly harder to endure. Even so, it's interesting that most of our social learning is geared toward penalizing or underestimating the value of self-love, maybe as a way of avoiding the clutches of vanity. If you decide to congratulate yourself with a kiss, it's likely that those around you (including the psychologist on duty) will label your behavior as ridiculous, narcissistic, or smug. It is frowned upon to like ourselves too much or to be really happy with who we are (someone who is very happy with themselves and with the world can easily be diagnosed as having hypomania, according to some renowned psychiatric classifications). When we spend too much time involved with ourselves, when we indulge or praise ourselves, the warnings come flooding in: "Be careful with an excess of self-esteem!" or "Watch out for too much pride!"

This is partly understandable given the havoc that can be wreaked by an inflated ego; however, it is one thing to be a narcissist (vainly obsessed with oneself), egotistical (selfish and incapable of loving others), or egocentric (incapable of recognizing different points of view), and totally another to be able to accept oneself honestly and genuinely without doing a song and dance about it. Humility is being aware of one's own shortcomings, but this in no way implies being ignorant of one's personal worth.

The catchphrase "Love yourself, but not in excess," meaning not irrationally or disproportionately (to avoid being entranced by your own self-image), is good advice because it makes us wary of the dark side of self-esteem. However, it's best not to exaggerate this and to be aware that, in certain situations where our self-love is taking a beating, loving ourselves without apprehension or irrational fears can get us back on track and allow us to walk with our heads held high.

Hiding and/or minimizing self-recognition and concealing our strengths causes more harm than good. The idea of not loving yourself "more than necessary" can turn into a kind of stifled and puny self-love. True, there's no need to shout at the top of our lungs about how wonderful we are, or splash it across the front pages, but repressing it, denying it, or contradicting it ends up hurting us emotionally. By trying to shut out unrestrained selfishness, we often fail to let in self-love; to avoid the insufferable pedantry of the know-it-all, some people succumb to shame about who they are; to avoid squandering, we are stingy. If I feel bad about exercising my personal rights or if I simply ignore them or believe that I do not deserve them, maybe I'm lacking some self-respect.

As we grow up, a strange insensitivity toward ourselves starts to take shape, leaving behind those glorious childhood days when the world seemed to revolve around us and we bounced happily from game to game. Back then, everything was gratifying and fanciful. At times, the self seemed to be enough on its own, giving itself pleasure and creating infinite universes at will (clearly, a child's natural inclination is not to punish themselves, but to have the best possible time and survive while they're at it). But good things don't last forever and, as we grow up, we leave behind that wonderful world of the self (as no society would survive under such egocentricity) and we look outward more than inward; in other words, we "decenter" and reluctantly accept that loving our neighbor is more important, worthy, and commendable than loving ourselves.

Current psychological findings on the issue of self-esteem are a warning worth heeding: We do not educate our children to love themselves, at least not in the organized and systematic way we teach them other things. From an early age, we are taught personal care habits regarding our physical self: brushing our teeth, bathing, cutting our nails, eating, controlling our bodily functions, dressing ourselves, and other similar activities, but what about *psychological care* and mental hygiene? Do we pay enough attention to that? Do we put it into practice? Do we highlight the importance of self-love?

THE FOUR PILLARS OF SELF-ESTEEM

The image you have of yourself is not hereditary or genetic, it is learned. The human brain has an information processing system that can store an almost infinite amount of data. That information, shaped by the social experiences of our lives, is stored in our long-term memory in the form of beliefs and theories. This provides us with internal models of objects, the meaning of words, situations, types of people, social activities, and much more. This knowledge of the world, correct or not, allows us to make predictions and prepare ourselves to face what is coming. The future is stored in the past.

The main source for creating your guiding worldview comes through contact with the people (friends, parents, teachers) from your immediate material and social surroundings. And the relationships you establish with your surrounding world develop within you an idea of how you believe you are. Successes and failures, fears and insecurities, physical sensations, pleasures and annoyances, the way you face problems, what people say to you and what they don't say to you, punishments and rewards, perceived love and rejection—all of this comes together and forms an internal image of your own persona; your "I" or self-schema. You can think that you are beautiful, efficient, interesting, intelligent, and good, or entirely the opposite (ugly, inefficient, boring, stupid, and bad). Each one of these value judgments is the result of a history in which you have been developing a "theory" about yourself, which will guide your behavior in the future. If you think that you are a loser, you will not try to win. You will say to yourself, "Why bother trying? I can't win" or "This isn't for me" or "I'm worthless."

We human beings have the conservative tendency toward confirming rather than debunking the beliefs we have stored in our brains for years. It is in our nature to resist change, and this mindset makes us stubborn and unreceptive to new stimuli. Once a belief has been established, it is difficult to change it, and it will be with you for the rest of your life if you do not make an effort to modify it. Furthermore, you will unconsciously do a number of things to prove these theories, even if they are harmful to you (that's how absurd we are as human beings). For example, if you get carried away with the mindset "I am useless," without realizing it, the fear of failure will lead you to make a multitude of mistakes, simply confirming the underlying mental opinion. The belief that you are ugly will make you hold back and avoid personal relationships, and the conquest for affection or sexual pleasure will become unattainable (nobody will notice you if you don't put yourself out there). A failure mindset will ensure that you do not dare to take on challenges or see if you are capable, leading you to believe that success evades you. There is no mysterious or quantum "secret" to this: In cognitive psychology it is known as a self-fulfilling prophecy, and as the Pygmalion effect in social psychology. There is a negative correlation: Even though you know it is not good for you, you will try to act in a way that fits the beliefs you have of yourself. Change? This will come about when reality prevails over your beliefs and you can no longer distort information and fool yourself. Good self-esteem (loving yourself convincingly) has several advantages, including allowing you to:

- *Increase positive emotions.* You will move away from anxiety, sadness, and depression, and move toward joy and the desire to live better.
- *Become more efficient in the tasks you take on.* You will not give up so easily, you will persevere in your goals and you will feel competent and capable.
- *Interact better with people.* You will overcome the fear of ridicule and the need for approval, because you will be the main judge of your behavior. It's not that you don't care about others, just that you will not be reliant on their applause and external support, and you will take criticism more objectively.

> *Be able to love your partner and your friends in a more relaxed manner.* You will be less dependent and establish more balanced and intelligent connections, without the terrible fear of losing others.
> *Be a more independent and autonomous person.* You will feel more freedom and security when making decisions and choosing your path.

The following are the four components that I consider to be the most important when shaping general self-esteem and, although in practice they are jumbled, for instructional purposes, I will try to separate them conceptually in order to better analyze them:

> *Self-concept* (what you think of yourself)
> *Self-image* (how much you like yourself)
> *Self-reinforcement* (how much you reward yourself)
> *Self-efficacy* (how much confidence you have in yourself)

Properly structured, these components are the four bases of a "solid and healthy self," and if they are not working, they become the Four Horsemen of the Apocalypse. If you fail at any of them, it will be enough to make your self-esteem lame and unstable. Furthermore, if just one of the Four Horsemen bolts, the other three will follow him like a small, out-of-control herd.

Healthy, properly constituted self-love is built on one fundamental principle: "I deserve anything that makes me grow as a person and makes me happy". D-e-s-e-r-v-e: articulated and savored. The activation of self-awareness and the well-being that comes with it. No matter what you think, you don't deserve to suffer, so if you can avoid useless and unnecessary suffering, you will be respecting yourself. There can be no complete happiness without self-respect, without staying true to your own self and the potential you carry within.

In each of the upcoming chapters, we will delve deep into each of the four components of self-esteem and how to improve them or maintain their strength.

CHAPTER 2

DEVELOP A GOOD SELF-CONCEPT

Have the courage to make mistakes.
—Hegel

Most of us walk around with an invisible and extremely painful club that we beat ourselves with every time we take a wrong turn or fail to reach our personal goals. Those who do not love themselves have learned to blame themselves for almost anything they do wrong and to doubt their own efforts when they do something right, as if they had their wires crossed. If they fail, they say, "That's on me," but if they manage to succeed at something, they say, "I was just lucky." There is a subculture of self-sabotage that negatively affects us and leads us to take more responsibility for bad things than good things. We shouldn't be so hard on ourselves.

Self-concept refers to what you think about yourself, to the concept you have of you as a person, just like you could have of someone else; therefore, this concept will be reflected in the way you treat yourself: what you say to yourself, what you demand from yourself, and how you do it. You can self-reinforce and reward yourself or you can insult yourself and fail to see the good in your behavior, or you can set yourself unattainable goals and chastise yourself for not reaching them. Although this might sound like the most irrational thing in the world, it is what many people do. We are victims of our own decisions. Each of us decides whether to love ourselves or not, even if we are not always aware of the damage we are doing to ourselves. As well as surviving fear and the daily struggle, we also need to learn how to survive ourselves: the enemy is not always out there.

BAD SELF-CRITICISM

Self-criticism is convenient and productive when done with care and with the goal of learning and growing. In the short-term, it can help to generate new behaviors and rectify errors, but if used indiscriminately and with cruelty, it will create stress and negatively affect our self-concept. If you use it incorrectly, you will end up thinking poorly of yourself no matter what you do. I have known people who "do not get along with themselves," do not accept themselves, and who reject themselves intensely ("I would like to be taller, better looking, smarter, more sensual, more efficient..." and the list is almost endless). They constantly compare themselves to those who are better than them or who surpass them in some way. You will frequently hear them say things like "I can't stand myself!" or "I'm a mess!" They replace the expression "It's better to be alone than in bad company" with "Bad company is better than no company." When I suggested to a young patient that she observe herself in order to get to know herself better, she panicked and said, "Just myself? But I can't stand myself even for a minute! I'm the most boring, uninteresting person on the planet!" Suggesting solitude created genuine terror in her because she didn't want to even think about being face-to-face with her own self.

The bad habit of constantly conducting harsh internal reviews increases dissatisfaction with oneself and feelings of insecurity. Nobody learns through methods based on punishment. As a child, I went to a school where the teaching methods were incredibly punitive. They treated us like potential criminals who had to be prosecuted and "educated at all costs." If you did not understand the class or did not do your homework correctly, they would sit you in the corner with a dunce cap and a pair of donkey ears (I'm not exaggerating one bit) and make you stare at the wall. The cruelty was exponential: Not only did they make you look totally useless in front of your classmates, they also literally exiled you from the rest of the class. I remember several times when I spent hours staring at the wall and counting ants. If you spoke in class or did something that went against the rules, the "corrective punishment" methods would force you to put your hands in the air so that the teacher could smack them with a ruler. (I repeat: everything happened in front of all the other students as a sort of "public chastisement.") The blows hurt a lot and, although they were not lashings, they felt like that. These humiliating methods were permitted by the school's board of directors and the Ministry of Education of the time.

This reminds me of a patient who did little but punish himself. He insulted himself about fifty times a day under his breath, he refrained from most pleasures, as if he were a fakir; he had so many rules and requirements for how to live that it was impossible for him to feel good. He was so limited and confused that he no longer knew who he really was. He would say that he felt like a photocopy of himself. And that is not an exaggeration: many people find that when they lose themselves in self-imposed duties and obligations, they no longer remember what they were really like. The psychological masks not only wear you out, they also depersonalize you. The man, who was only thirty-five, was incapable of making decisions for himself and would almost seek permission just to breathe. My patient had grown up with the idea that if he did not strictly adhere to the rules he had been taught, he would stop being a good person. This is too heavy a burden for any person, which begs the question: How did he survive such regulatory suffocation? To manage self-imposed repression, he developed three methods: excessive self-control, obsessive self-observation, and ruthless self-criticism. Three lethal weapons. Punishing himself made him feel good, correct, and "saved." When he sought professional help and embarked on his own "moral-psychological revolution," he came to the healthy conclusion that he did not deserve to mistreat himself. He began to allow himself some nice indiscretions, such as eating a triple chocolate ice cream with whipped cream without worrying about the indulgence, dressing well without feeling vain or guilty, or noticing a woman on the street without feeling lecherous.

Systematic punishment, in any of its forms, will only teach you to flee from the predators and punishers of the moment; to run away, nothing more. You will not solve or face the underlying problem. But when we talk about self-punishment, the problem is that you are the executioner, so you will bear it on your shoulders like a burden: defending yourself becomes like trying to escape your own shadow. Countless people have a self-evaluation system that makes them suffer day and night, every moment, and which, inexplicably, makes them feel proud of the martyr they have made of themselves.

SELF-LABELING: "I AM" OR "I BEHAVED"?

A variation on harmful self-criticism *is negative self-labeling*: hanging signs that speak poorly of you or letting (and accepting) others hang them to place you in a category that harms you. Social classifications (stereotypes) tend to refer to others in global, unspecific terms, without taking into account exceptions or extenuating circumstances. The same thing happens when you negatively label yourself: you confuse the part with the whole. Instead of saying "I acted awkwardly," you will say "I am awkward." Or "I am useless" instead of saying "I messed up with this or that." It is not the same thing to say, "I am not eating well" than to say, "I am a pig." The large-scale, cutting, and definitive attack on your own "self," on what you are, creates all kinds of imbalances and alterations. On the other hand, constructive self-criticism is precise and never goes to the depth of the entire being. If you told the person that you love, "You're wrong, you are an idiot!" how would they feel? How would they react? You would cause them harm, wouldn't you? Well, similarly, attacking your self-worth, punching your value, affects you psychologically much more than you think.

RUTHLESS DEMANDS OF YOURSELF

Other people demonstrate the tendency to use unattainable internal standards to evaluate themselves.

In other words, they use disproportionate goals and criteria for what their behavior should look like. If self-demand is rational and well calculated, it can help you to progress psychologically, but if it is unmeasured, it can seriously affect your mental health. Both extremes are bad. Nobody can deny that there are times when we need moderate or elevated levels of self-discipline to be competent (for example, the person in charge of handling radioactive material in a nuclear power plant cannot do it with carefree abandon, just like a surgeon operating on a patient); however, the imbalance occurs when these levels of discipline are impossible to attain. For example, the idea that I should excel in almost everything I do, that I should be the best at all costs, and that I should not make mistakes is a demand that can be truly agonizing. If happiness or self-realization is based solely on obtaining results, you will soon discover the paradox that "to feel good" you must "feel bad." Well-being will depend on so many factors outside yourself that it will be impossible for you to be responsible for your personal achievements. The poet Margaret Lee Runbeck once said, "Happiness is not a station you arrive at, but a manner of traveling." That is mental health: traveling well.

Those who are obsessed with success, who place too much worth on it, and who have strict performance self-schema travel poorly even though they want it to appear otherwise. Perhaps happiness does not lie in being the best salesperson, the best mother, the best son, or in standing out in everything, but simply in *trying* honestly and calmly, in enjoying it while doing it, in taking in the surroundings while going where you want to go. Have you ever been on a trip with someone who is constantly asking how much longer until you arrive, while ignoring all the beautiful things they are passing?

Focusing on the process is vital to obtaining a good end product. This apparent contradiction (not worrying about the result in order to achieve it) is actually not a contradiction, it is well demonstrated by the Zen teaching of the bow and arrow. If the archer concentrates on his movements, his breathing, his balance, instead of focusing on hitting the target, he will do just that simply by aiming. But if hitting the bullseye and getting the highest score becomes the main issue (obsessive), anxiety will block the flow of his movements and he will fail. If you have strict criteria for self-evaluation, you will always feel insufficient, as if you haven't hit the target. Your body will start to secrete more adrenaline than normal and physical and mental tension will interfere with your performance: you will enter the vicious cycle of those who want more but have less each day.

This self-destructive sequence is better illustrated in the following image:

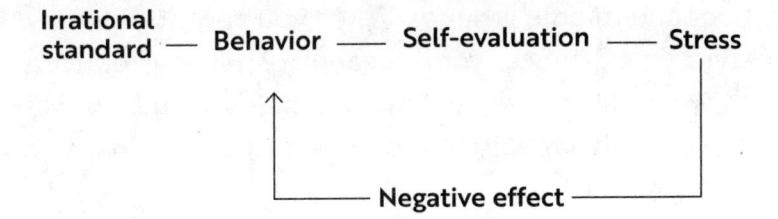

```
Irrational
standard ── Behavior ──── Self-evaluation ──── Stress
                    ↑                                │
                    └──────── Negative effect ───────┘
```

Impossible goals will mean that your behavior will never reach the desired level, despite your efforts, and feeling incompetent will ensure that your self-evaluation will become increasingly negative, and your stress levels will be higher, distancing you further from your objectives. Isn't that just nonsense?

People who get caught in this trap become depressed, lose control of their own behavior, and inevitably make mistakes. Precisely what they were trying to avoid! The premise is the more you make of "earning" a value, the more destined you will be to fail.

ALL OR NOTHING

Those who demand a lot of themselves have a dichotomous way of processing information. For them, life is black and white, with no gray areas. "I am successful or I am a failure," "I am capable or incapable," "I am intelligent or stupid." This way of thinking is mistaken, because there is nothing absolute or firmly at one extreme. If we see the world this way, we stop perceiving hues and middle grounds. When you apply this binary style to existence, your vocabulary will be reduced to words like *never, always, all,* or *nothing*. You will collide with a reality that differs vastly from what you imagine.

The inability to consider other paths and the fear of losing or not reaching your objectives will mean that you ignore any approximations to your personal goals. For those who live in the "all or nothing" world, making progress is not seen or felt, or it simply goes by unnoticed. They will say, "I have or I haven't reached my goal." They see the tree, but not the forest.

CHANGE AND REVISION

Changing is not an easy task. Not only because it implies a personal effort, but also because of the social costs. If someone makes the brave decision to "travel well" and step outside of the established patterns, the social pressure will be inescapable, especially when the individual's goals do not align with the values of their reference group. For example, in some subcultures, those vocational objectives that are removed from economic gains are seen as synonymous with laziness or naïve idealism. In one session, a lady said to me, "I want you to evaluate my son… something weird is going on with him. He wants to study music instead of engineering!" When we stray from the conventional path to take a more daring one, and when we take new roads, unyielding people who stick to norms will label us as "immature" or "unstable," as if "not changing direction" were synonymous with intelligence. A quick look at the people who have played an important role in the history of humanity shows that the existence of a certain "instability" and lack of satisfaction with the prevailing living conditions are essential conditions for living intensely. Radical conformity or absolute composure are bastions that do not shake the world. Don't be afraid to review, change, or modify your goals if they are a source of suffering. How else can you move closer to happiness?

So the important thing is not only to manage suitable levels of self-demand (nonharmful), but also to be able to review and modify the criteria that is suffocating you and stopping you from being who you want to be. To do this, you cannot be too "stable" or "structured," you need a pinch of "insanity" or "motivational madness," in a good sense. Those who are very self-critical or strict with themselves tend to suffer a lot because the world does not fit their expectations. They have created so many conditions and requirements for their journey through life that they crash into the walls of irrational normativity and duties at every turn. In turn, others travel along a truly comfortable and tranquil highway: *Being flexible and self-evaluating is undoubtedly a virtue of those who are emotionally and rationally intelligent.*

Those who do not accept themselves are strangely invested in the rules that determine emotional survival: they are too "hard" on themselves when critiquing their own performance and too "soft" when evaluating others. On the contrary, according to available data, subjects who show high levels of self-esteem try to maintain a fair balance when evaluating themselves; they don't destroy themselves or others. In no way am I defending sustained self-deception; I simply think that it is very useful for mental health to "turn the other cheek" to small, insignificant errors and personal flaws. We have to pamper the "self". The foolishness of the alternative is evident: Those who are too strict with themselves simply place a straitjacket on themselves to avoid becoming unhinged, but the result tends to be a psychological imbalance.

SAVING YOUR SELF-CONCEPT

The following is a guide that could help you protect your self-concept from self-punishment, self-criticism, and indiscriminate demands on yourself.

1. Try to Be More Flexible with Yourself and Others

Try not to use extreme dichotomous criteria to evaluate reality or yourself. Do not think in absolute terms because there is nothing that is totally good or bad. It is better to be tolerant of the fact that things sometimes go off track and not to lose sleep over it. I know it hurts, but the world does not revolve around you, and your wishes are not the desire of the universe (the cosmos is not that submissive). Learn to accept discrepancies and to understand your rigidity as a defect, not a virtue: having the last word or imposing your point of view is nothing more than bravado. Rigid things are less malleable, they cannot handle the variable nature of the world that contains them, and they get fractured. If you follow the rules, if you are a perfectionist and intolerant, you won't know what to do with life, because life is not like that. This will result in most daily events causing you stress, because they aren't the same as how you would like them to be. This type of stress has a name: "low frustration tolerance."

Make the effort to focus on the nuances for a week or two. Do not rush to categorize definitively. Stop and consider whether what you are saying is really true. Review the way you refer to people and yourself; don't be drastic. Consider the people around you that you have already categorized and dedicate some time to questioning the sign you've hung around their neck, look for evidence to counter this, discover the middle ground, and, when evaluating, avoid using words like *always, never, all,* or *nothing*. As a renowned psychologist observed, saying "he stole once" is not the same as saying, "he is a robber." People "are," but they can also "behave" in certain ways. It's time for you to rip apart your rigidity because inflexibility creates hate and unease.

The following points can help to sum this up:

a. *Try not to be a perfectionist.*
Mess with your routine, your rituals, your journeys, and the way you arrange things, as if it were a game, just to see what happens. Live with the chaos for a week and do not fear it. You will discover that everything remains more or less the same and so much effort to control things was a waste of time.

b. *Do not label people or yourself.*
Try to be kind, especially to yourself. Only speak in terms of behaviors when you refer to someone or your "self."

c. *Focus on the nuances.*
Focus more on the alternatives and exceptions to the rule. Life is made up of more hues and colors than just black and white.

d. *Listen to people who think differently from you.*
This does not necessarily mean that you need to change your opinion, just listen. Let the information in and then decide.

Remember: If you are inflexible and rigid with the world and with people, you will end up being like that with yourself. You won't forgive the slightest fault and will end up being your own executioner.

2. Review Your Goals and the Realistic Chances of Reaching Them

Please, don't set unattainable goals for yourself! Make demands of yourself in line with your real abilities and possibilities. If you find yourself trying to climb a figurative Mount Everest and it is causing you anguish, you have two rational options: choose a different mountain or just enjoy the journey. When you set a goal, you should also set the steps to get there, or subgoals. Try to savor going up each step, as if each one were a higher objective in itself, independent of the summit. Don't wait until you reach the top before resting or enjoying the journey or the effort. Look for intermediate breaks and lose yourself in them for a while, in the nooks and crannies and roads that don't lead to Rome. Write down your goals, review them, question them, and discard those that aren't vital and that don't come from within you. Life is too short to waste on an uncertain path, or one imposed by ideals that aren't born from your soul or are imposed from outside and alien to your being.

Remember, if your goals are unattainable, you will spend your life frustrated and bitter. Nobody will be able to put up with you, not even you.

3. Don't Just See the Bad in Yourself

If you only focus on your mistakes, you won't see your achievements. If you only see what is missing, you won't enjoy the moment, the here and now. Tagore once said, "If you cry because the sun has gone out of your life, your tears will prevent you from seeing the stars." There are times when our heart knows or grasps more information than our grim reason. Don't just be aware of your failures, also try to turn your attention to your good behavior, that which is productive, albeit imperfect. The method I would suggest is to redirect your attention in a kind and balanced way: When you find yourself negatively and excessively focusing on your "bad behavior or thoughts," stop! Take a breath and try to tip the scales. Don't take pleasure in the suffering.

4. Don't Think Poorly of Yourself

Be kinder with your actions. Fortunately, you are neither perfect nor that horrible, although you insist on believing you are. Don't insult or disrespect yourself. Keep a record of your negative self-evaluations, see which ones are fair, moderate, and objective, and which ones are not; and if you find that the language used about yourself is offensive, change it and find more constructive and respectful value judgements for yourself. Reduce your self-verbalizations (thoughts about yourself) to those that are really worth it, and exercise your right to make mistakes. Human beings, like animals, learn by trial and error, even if some people believe that human learning should be done through "trial and success" (this is false, and possibly the product of a narcissistic mind). Growing as a human being involves getting things wrong and "screwing up": this is an inescapable universal law. It's impossible not to be wrong from time to time, so there is nothing you can do but humbly accept this without throwing a tantrum. What you need to understand is that errors do not make you better or worse, they simply toughen you, show you new options, and drag you by the hair to a truth that is not always pleasant: they just remind you that you are human. When we discuss self-efficacy, we will speak again about the fear of making a mistake; for now, you just need to understand a basic principle of mental health: if you err, don't treat yourself badly.

5. Love Yourself for as Much Time as Possible

That would be ideal. Stable self-love is preferable to one that fluctuates and depends on external factors (stable self-esteem, controlled by you). The premise, "If it goes wrong, I hate myself, and if it goes well, I love myself," is unfair on you. Would you do the same with your son or daughter? No, right? You would love your children despite everything and above everyone else. You would educate them, sure, but your affection for them would not change based on their results, it wouldn't change one bit. If the love you have for yourself fluctuates too much or depends on your feats and great achievements, maybe you don't love yourself that much. It's worth clarifying that, although proper self-esteem is steady over time and tends to be constant, that does not mean there will not be times when you feel a surge of fleeting "mini-hate" toward yourself for what you did or did not do, and you might even find that you can't stand yourself for a few hours. You will grumble, throw tantrums, and have arguments between "me" and "me," but your personal worth, if you really love yourself, will never be at stake. You will forgive yourself and your idyllic romance will rekindle with aplomb. However, if the fluctuations between self-love and hate are regular, you should seek professional help.

6. Try to Move Your "Ideal Me" Closer to Your "Real Me"

Impossible and extremely rigid goals increase the gap between your ideal me (what you would like to do or be) and your real me (what you actually do or are). The greater the distance between the two, the lower the chance of meeting your objective and the more frustration and insecurity you will feel. You won't love yourself, you will not calmly accept who you really are, you will see the imaginary "other me," someone who does not exist. If you have idealized who you should be too much, who you really are will annoy you, and, according to my experience as a therapist, the only tool you will have to improve yourself will be to accept who you are, without anesthesia and without deceiving yourself. Maybe there are a lot of things you don't like about yourself, but the important thing is the raw material, which often passes you by and you are unable to observe because you are fixated on the dream "self" that's living in the clouds.

7. Learn to Lose

Exaggerated self-demands are measured according to your possibilities, it's as simple as that. If you do not have the skills or resources needed to achieve your goals, even the simplest aspiration will become torturous. In these cases, an objective and frank reevaluation of your aspirations, considering your abilities, is the solution: *You have to learn how to lose.* There is a healthy resignation when facts prevail and you can look at them objectively: stubbornly persisting toward a goal can become a problem. Sometimes we have to wake up from our dreams, because they will not become reality, and that does not make you better or worse, just more realistic and grounded. Laying down your weapons and understanding that the battle is no longer yours will make you feel freer and happier and a better fighter in life.

Let's recap and clarify some things. Moderate self-criticism, objective self-observation, constructive self-evaluation, and rational and reasonable goals help develop our human potential. I am not denouncing self-criticism and self-demand *per se* and in all circumstances. What I maintain is that in order to escape a harmful psychological extreme (a poor spirit, laziness, failure, feeling worthless, and not having any expectations of growth), we sometimes swing the pendulum to the other extreme, which is equally damaging and harmful. You are a special machine within a known universe, do not mistreat or insult yourself. To be successful you do not need to punish yourself.

CHAPTER 3

DEVELOP A GOOD SELF-IMAGE

*Life consists not in holding good cards,
but in playing those you hold well.*
—Josh Billings

In almost every era and culture, physical beauty has been admired as a special gift, and unattractiveness as a curse from nature or the gods. We must be aware that a lot of people are especially cruel to those who fall outside the traditional standards of what is considered beautiful, often going so far as to reject them. You just need to look at the way that some children laugh at their peers who are overweight or excessively skinny, those who are very short or very tall, or generally those who have some sort of disproportionate trait. Even people who are unfortunate enough to suffer from physical deformities are victims of attacks on their appearance. Whatever it may be, the form the molecular structure of our body adopts is a source of attraction or repulsion (social conventions are unforgiving). The exclusive premise is this: "These are the established parameters, and if you do not meet them, you won't get into the lucky people's club."

What we should be concerned about is that the culturally imposed judgment of physical appearance has enormous consequences for our future. As highlighted in several studies, success in several different areas of performance is affected by physical attractiveness. Although it is unfair and should not be that way, data shows that judgments of beautiful people are kinder. That said, there is no universal criteria for beauty. The ideal of what is beautiful is learned through personal and social experiences in our immediate surroundings and the ideas that social conventions and the media instill in us.

THE WEIGHT OF COMPARISON

As I have mentioned, our closest reference group and the relationships we establish with people are determining factors in the creation of the idea we have of our body and the evaluations we make of it (self-image). The "Ugly Duckling" story is not pure fiction. I have met countless families who consider physical beauty to be a value, and if any of the children do not meet the characteristics of what they consider "beautiful," they simply fail to form an affectionate bond with them. They can't kick them out entirely (blood is thicker than water), but they are unable to integrate entirely into the family/emotional nucleus in the same way that good-looking people can. This "aesthetic distancing" is subtle and plagued by compensatory consolations, like saying, "She isn't that pretty, but she has other good qualities."

All the while, children observe, process, and absorb the differing treatment and signs of admiration that come from poorly hidden comparisons. As if that wasn't enough, "pro-beauty" families not only instill the need to be beautiful in the child, they also place body image at unattainable levels. In my professional experience, I have seen people who do not accept themselves because they consider themselves "ugly" or "unpleasant," even though they aren't, because they fail to meet the aesthetic ideal held by their reference group (parents, friends, or social circle).

One of my patients held the firm conviction that she was not attractive, despite actually being a beautiful and interesting woman. Despite the persuasive efforts of the therapy group, her belief was unshakeable: "Doctor," she would say, "I sincerely thank you for your efforts, and I know that you would never tell me that I'm ugly because that would depress me even more…" To test her irrational belief and the resulting distorted view of her physical appearance, I designed a typical attitude-gauging experiment. The patient sat in the cafeteria of a busy university next to two attractive women, chosen by her, who acted as comparison subjects. A group of one hundred students, male and female, was asked to evaluate the beauty and sensuality of the patient and the two other women she had chosen, on a scale of one to ten. Once the data was processed, it was discovered that around 90 percent of the observers had the opinion that she was a beautiful, sensual, attractive, and desirable person. Upon seeing the results, the patient was surprised. She thought for a while and then said, "It's incredible... I don't know what to say... I never would have thought that people had such bad taste!" Her belief in her imperfection had taken her to the extreme of ignoring and distorting any information that proved her wrong.

THE PERSONAL MAGNIFYING GLASS

For some strange reason, nicknames always tend to hit where it hurts. Physical defects have the unique quality of being immediately detectable by others, however small they might be. And even if a positive change occurs over the years, such as the supposed "defect" disappearing or being treated medically, the ridicule leaves its mark and becomes an evaluation criterion that we apply to ourselves. As we grow up and learn what is "beautiful" and "ugly," we no longer need people to tell us, we can just look in the mirror. Particularly in preadolescence and adolescence, we begin a detailed and almost compulsive review of what we are physically—point by point, pore by pore, part by part. The result is that few things make the grade and we are almost always missing or exceeding in something. We criticize our skin color, our hair, our teeth, our eyes, our legs, our fingers, or any other thing that doesn't pass the filter, even things that aren't exposed to the public! I remember a patient who refused to go to the beach because his toes were too big and crooked. One day he took his shoes off and showed them to me. I was expecting to be greeted by something like the paws of a werewolf, but honestly, if he had not explained to me in great detail the alleged "imperfection," I never would have batted an eyelid. His fear was that women wouldn't like him because of the "anomaly." My response was simple: I told him that if a woman rejected him because one of his toes was two or three millimeters longer than another, he should find someone else.

Some people have an astonishing ability to detect faults in themselves and blow them out of proportion (in extreme cases, like that of my patient, this type of understanding is known as body dysmorphic disorder and it requires proper professional help).

MIRROR, MIRROR...

I am not criticizing personal care or grooming, given that it is only natural that we would want to look good and attract others and ourselves, rather I am against the obsessive desire to be "beautiful" all the time, according to the current experts. This type of personal self-affirmation—in other words, something expressed as "my value as a human being depends on my physical beauty"—indicates an alarming reversal of essential values. The same thing applies to those who demonstrate the overriding need to maintain their youth and beauty above all else and do not understand that each age has its "charm." If what we see in the mirror does not meet the aesthetic ideal that we have learned (what we would like to see), we will never feel good about our body. A patient, an actor who often played the heartthrob, used to tell me, "It would be better to live in a world without clocks or mirrors—not worry about how time passes, with no past to regret (our lost youth) and no future to fear (the inevitable wrinkles and old age)." I responded that, in any case, other people would notice and, sooner or later, they would point out new gray hairs and extra pounds. We have to grow old, there's no escaping that. You don't need to be a Buddhist to understand it and accept it; the idea is to do it with elegance and dignity.

INVENTING BEAUTY

Most people will accept the fact that there are no universal and absolute criteria for what constitutes being beautiful. I remember my grandmother would always talk about her mother as if she were the most beautiful and attractive person in the world, following some standards that must have outraged more than one aesthetic doctor. "How beautiful my mother was!" she would say. "Chubby, white as snow, with rosy cheeks, and lips as red as strawberries." When she would say this, all of us grandkids would roll around on the floor laughing, with the eldest among us grimacing. Today, those "ancient" standards of beauty do not fit in our mental structures. It isn't easy for postmodern thinking to "process" the attractive qualities of silent movies stars, Miss Universe from fifty years ago, or the "statuesque" bodies of the 1960s. This relativity is evident in other areas too. For example, the Iesus Indigenous people of Guatemala favor large, strong women, because they can carry firewood and do difficult physical tasks: that is their sex appeal. The premise is clear: *Beauty is something relative to the time and the place,* even if certain biological variables come into play. The idea of what should be considered "beautiful" or "horrifying" is instilled in and taught to us, but this is by no means an absolute truth. In my great-grandmother's time, beauty criteria revolved around being well-fed, while today it is signs of malnutrition that get paraded along catwalks and earn admiration and envy.

The healthiest way to look at it is this: you can choose your own concept of beauty. It isn't easy, but it's worth a try. Just as you don't need to blindly follow fashion and wear a uniform to dress well, you don't need to rely on external concepts to be attractive to yourself. You don't need to look like anyone in particular, and there are no theoretical or scientific reasons that justify the superiority of one form of beauty over others.

The requirements for your aesthetic preferences are basically a complex mix of cognitive and emotional variables, perhaps more of the latter; this is why, often, when we meet a person who "we like," with whom "there is chemistry," we cannot explain precisely what it is that attracts us. I have met racist people in love with a person of color, communists in love with affluent people, anarchists in love with police officers, and makeup artists in love with people with unfixable skin. The aesthetic-attraction contradiction is in the hands of some as-yet-unknown natural mechanism that pushes us toward someone that does not meet our demands of what is beautiful, but who attracts us despite everything. If social convention had been kinder in its aesthetic rules, beauty pageants would not exist and all the companies that revolve around the obsession with the body would go broke.

So the important thing is not to be beautiful, but to be attractive to oneself. The best way to do this is to avoid previously established standards and instead invent your own. Beauty is an attitude: If you feel beautiful, you are beautiful, and you will communicate that to others, but if you accept the model of beauty that is imposed on you from the outside, you will end up thinking you are ghastly. I'm sure you've experienced the unpleasant sensation of feeling terrible about yourself after seeing a commercial filled with models who have had every kind of surgery. What to do? The healthiest response is to highlight the things that you really like about yourself, even if they don't match with the general "vibe." One of my patients turned the supposed pleasure of buying clothes into genuine torture. "Doctor," she would say, "I get stressed out because I don't know what I should buy." I would reply, "Whatever you like." And she would respond, "And how do I know that my taste is the right one?" It took a lot of work for me to make her understand there are no errors when it comes to taste or, as the saying goes, "different strokes."

I repeat: Your body and the way you choose to cover it should first and foremost be appealing to you. "Decorate yourself" at your whim and to your taste; in other words, however you want. If you don't do that, your decisive power will be at the mercy of what "people wear" and what "people don't wear." For example, feeling well-dressed is something nice (I've sometimes thought that the greatest happiness shared by wedding guests, including relatives, is not the joy of those getting married, but the feeling of being elegant), but being obsessed with "how I look" can be an exhausting and tiring task.

IMPROVING YOUR SELF-IMAGE

To safeguard or rescue your self-image, you need to consider the following points.

1. Try to Define Your Own Beauty or Aesthetic Criteria

Don't get carried away by "expert" opinions: nobody knows anything about this. Don't let those who criticize your preferences affect you either; it is a choice that only you can make. Trust in your instinctive tastes and take a chance on trying out your own fashion. Answer the stupid question, "Do people wear this?" with the simple answer, "I have no idea." Much to your dismay, you will discover that people will begin to see you as a "role model." Dress up for yourself and not for others.

2. Discard Physical Perfection and Strict Criteria

Don't become trapped by unattainable ideals. There is no absolute when it comes to beauty, which is why you will find there are people who are attracted to someone that you aren't even remotely attracted to. Don't waste time pondering what you need to be Aphrodite or Adonis, just enjoy what you have, play your cards right and don't demand the impossible of yourself. The idea of physical perfection will only lead you to focus your attention on your defects and to forget your qualities. So you aren't aesthetically perfect? Welcome to the world of normal people! I have met women and men whose egos don't even fit in their bodies, who spend hours at the gym, and who feel special and physically entrancing; they don't walk, they strut. Recently, I saw some graffiti in Barcelona that said: "Beauty is in your head." I would say that it is in two heads: in the head that looks and evaluates, and in the one that puts itself out there. Get your head out of the clouds. Your anatomical physique is not important, it's how you carry it.

3. Discover and Highlight the Things You Like about Yourself

Sometimes, when we detect some unpleasant aspect of our physical appearance, a sort of generalized dazzling effect is produced, as if that sole feature had stupefied us and we couldn't see anything else. An annoying mole, an unexpected dark spot, a slightly lower ear, dull hair, and so on. The important thing here is to expand your attention to also include what you like about you and to decrease the insufferable glare of what you do not like, which stops you from enjoying what is pleasing. No matter how many or few positive physical attributes you have, be glad that you have them and enjoy them. You are lucky to have them! They are yours! Never think that you have "run out" of charming qualities: explore and you will be surprised by the interesting, seductive, and sensual things you can find in yourself, that have nothing to do with proportions. A young woman once worriedly said to me, "I don't know why he chose me when there are other much more beautiful women." In fact, she was right. There will always be someone more handsome or prettier than you. But that isn't everything! My patient had an infectious smile, a mischievous look in her eyes and an enchanting personality. She was also incredibly intelligent and she knew how to carry herself with poise and confidence. People don't fall in love with a pair of calves, a fibula, or a tibia, they fall in love with the person who carries them!

4. *Your Self-Image Is Communicated to Others*

If you feel like a boring and unattractive person, you will portray this image to others and they will treat you that way, which will confirm your belief. They might even discriminate against you and you will fall deeper into a dark and sad view of yourself. As I've said, in certain ways, beauty is an attitude. If you pity yourself, others will pity you; if you feel sorry for yourself, others will feel sorry for you; if you see yourself as unlikeable, they will reject you. You create your own interpersonal context: your space for growth or your niche. The best way to break this negative circle is to like yourself and end this defect/shame model that you have been carrying around for years, even if it is mild. Try playing the role of someone who is satisfied with their body and see how you feel. Test this behavior for a while, feel irresistible, and try to act that way, without becoming annoying, obviously. "Here I am, this is what I am, and if you don't like it, I'm sorry." The circle will begin to crumble. I'm not talking about vanity, but about the emotional survival that comes from being a little more pleasant about your physical appearance. Look around you and tell me how many people you know are married to or in a relationship with supermodels or divas. Most of us veer on the average or even tend to be a little ugly; and that's the advantage: We are the majority, so there is a greater chance of meeting someone like us—in other words, imperfect.

5. Physical Appearance Is Only One Part of Self-Image

Reinforcing the previous point, being good-looking is just one factor of who you are as a person. Your essence goes way beyond that. After a couple of hours, your physical attributes are not even the most important part of attraction. Aside from being "beautiful" or "ugly," people can also be warm, kind, smart, sweet, seductive, sensual, interesting, polite, jolly, affectionate, funny, stupid, and tons of other things. There are people who just have the "spark" and that is a crucial ingredient in forming relationships. In other words, you have a lot of different options for things to like about yourself and reasons to stop insulting yourself every time you look in the mirror. Once again, I'm not saying you should neglect your body—or your appearance—but you should only give it the attention it deserves. Ask yourself what else you are made of apart from skin and bones. And if you can't find anything, seek professional help.

6. Don't Magnify What You Don't Like about Yourself

I'm talking about the invisible magnifying glass that we sometimes carry around, that makes a small pimple look like a mountain or a tiny imperfection appear to be an almost monstrous anomaly, magnifying unpleasant things until, like an avalanche, they bury all the pleasant features and everything becomes contaminated. Focusing our attention on what we like least, and exaggerating it, leads us to believe that salvation is impossible and we should just remove ourselves from the rest of the world. A patient once told me, "I'm here because I'm worried about going bald." I thought it was a joke when I looked at this man's full, lustrous head of hair. He had long, black, shiny hair—it really was enviable. When I asked him what his anguish was based on, he lifted up a few strands of hair and pointed to a circle of about three millimeters in diameter above his temples, where the amount of hair was less than in other parts. Then he said that the dermatologist had told him it was nothing to worry about and didn't even prescribe him anything. However, he was stuck on the idea that he was at the serious onset of baldness and spent the whole time pushing his hair forward to cover the "unpopulated area" that only he could see. It took a lot of work to get him to stop using the magnifying glass that he had created and to learn to focus on his positive attributes in other areas: for example, those inside rather than on his head.

7. There Will Always Be Someone Willing to Love You

If you truly like and accept yourself, you will always find someone who likes you and is capable of loving you. Disliking oneself blocks the ability to form relationships because people who are not happy with their bodies anticipate rejection and avoid others. They are fearful of a negative evaluation and their levels of social anxiety go through the roof. Flirting and seduction do not even cross their minds because they consider themselves to look ridiculous in such a situation. They never take the first step and, if somebody approaches them, they chase them away with their insecurities and precaution.

Liking yourself is expanding your romantic horizons: How can you love someone who does not love themselves? If you do not like yourself, you will never be able to process, accept, or take the affection that people naturally and happily offer you.

8. Don't Make Unfair Comparisons

Don't be cruel to yourself. Don't compare yourself as if you were an item for sale. Making comparisons is hateful, but it is even more unfair if you are using the "top" people in any area as a reference. Those who compare themselves with the best, the most successful, the most famous, just any of the "most," spend their lives bitter about what they "are not" or "are missing." An older woman once told me, "When I am walking down the street, I just see young and beautiful women and that makes me feel old and ugly." Obviously! She would also buy her clothes in youth fashion stores, where nothing fit her, and she spent her time in the hands of an aesthetic practitioner who took as many years as possible off her. Her mind's time was spent thinking about how to turn back time. This masochistic attitude was backed by the collection of anti-values that she wasn't even conscious of (obsession takes away clarity).

Even if your expectations are in the clouds, you simply must admit it: there are people who are younger, smarter, richer, more famous, and more beautiful than you. Each of us has our charm and you have yours. Some people find solace by looking at people who are below them in terms of aesthetic statistics and conclude that they aren't "that ugly." This consolation tactic might keep your self-esteem afloat sometimes, but it is not good for your personal growth because it doesn't make you face what you are. It's better not to compare yourself at all and to accept yourself unconditionally, to love yourself, to spruce yourself up; neither by defect nor by excess, without reference points above or below (if there even is an above and below). For your self-esteem to function properly, there must be an approval of the essence, an admission of the basics, an alignment with your own "self," including your body. When you fall in love, you don't do it "just a little bit," you either love or you don't love. The same applies when the affection is aimed at yourself. You love yourself or you don't, you accept yourself or you don't.

CHAPTER 4

DEVELOP GOOD SELF-REINFORCEMENT

> *Once in a century a man may be ruined or made insufferable by praise. But surely once in a minute something generous dies for want of it.*
>
> —John Masefield

If someone were to say, "My partner rarely compliments me, they don't usually indulge me, they aren't concerned about my health, they hardly dedicate any time to me, and they almost never show me affection," we would surely agree that the existence of a real feeling of love is doubtful. In the same way, if you never build yourself up or reward yourself, if you don't dedicate any time to you, if you don't show yourself any affection, your self-esteem will basically be nonexistent. Self-love, in principle, should not be that different from loving others, at least in terms of its basic modus operandi.

If we are responsible and sensible and we carefully plan our commitments, work schedules, budgets, and the like, why don't we do the same when it comes to managing our self-reinforcements? For example, why is free time remnant, a "leftover" once all our obligations are done, and then we often don't even know what to do with it? We run around at 100 miles per hour and every now and again we stop to relax and enjoy some leisure time. What happened to those years of our childhood and youth when we would "let time go by" without fear or guilt? There's no space in our planner! For those who live to work, rest has been reduced to a passive function for recovering our strength. When night falls, work addicts do not sleep, they pass out!

We have time for our children, partners, parents, in-laws, neighbors, friends, but it doesn't cross our mind to spend some free time for our own benefit, and alone! We aren't as interested in generating mental health as we are in earning money. Many of my patients feel guilty when I manage to convince them to sit under a tree and do nothing but admire nature and play with the grass. It does not take long for irrational thoughts like "I'm wasting time" to appear. The argument is that "if time is money, I'm losing money." The fear of falling prey to leisure and laziness has developed such an absurd hyperactive behavioral pattern that we are unable to stop being "dynamic" and "hard-working" all the time. Things like thinking, dreaming, fantasizing, sleeping, meditating, or gazing for the sake of gazing are seen as a way of frittering away our lives or simply being idle. People who think like that will have serious trouble loving themselves peacefully, as their thoughts will always focus on being able to do something "more productive" than just having a good time.

It is absurd to think that our own "self" ranks last in the expressions of affection we are capable of giving. We spend our time putting off the rewards that we deserve and telling ourselves, "One day I'm going to do it," but that day rarely arrives. "I'll start tomorrow" + "I'll start tomorrow" + "I'll start tomorrow" = procrastination. A patient who loved music once told me that they had bought a saxophone for when they retired. "I will have free time," they said, "to play what I want." I was really concerned by this postponement and told them that when they were old and retired, they probably would not have enough air in their lungs to blow.

From an early age, we are instilled with the idea that self-control and the postponement of pleasure are traits that differentiate us from less evolved animals. But this should not be taken completely at face value: postponing certain pleasures or triggers can be an important skill in a diet, when we quit smoking or try to be less aggressive, but if we make putting off healthy pleasure a way of life, we will be playing into the hands of depression and our existence will slowly lose its positive side. The cost will be insensitivity and the loss of the ability to be amazed. Constantly having the emergency brake on, in an attempt to be prudent, appropriate, convenient, measured, and sensible, will lead you to emotional lethargy and absolute apathy for the things that could bring you closer to a fuller life. You will lose the ability to vibrate and get excited, you will create a shield and get used to routine, fun and happiness will seem bothersome to you.

Many people feel irresponsible if they go overboard or "fall" into certain totally harmless temptations, like indulging themselves. They have simply created the irrational and restrictive belief that rewarding themselves is a highly dangerous, narcissistic "vice," so they stay within healthy and inoffensive limits.

HEDONISTIC PHILOSOPHY

Hedonism means pleasure, satisfaction, delight, enjoyment, and well-being. A hedonistic philosophy implies a lifestyle geared toward seeking pleasure and making the most of the things that surround us, obviously without being a slave to them or becoming a victim of addiction. A guiding premise you could use is the following: "If it isn't harmful to you or others, you can do whatever you want." Having a good time and enjoying life does not mean, as some people believe, falling into an orgy of uncontrolled behavior without a hint of mental organization. A hedonistic person is not a superficial, morally corrupt being who only seeks out the mundane pleasure of eating and drinking (you just need to read Epicurius to understand this). Someone who follows a responsible hedonistic philosophy does not avoid the daily struggle and problems, they are simply aware of what makes them happy and actively work toward getting and intensely enjoying it. Between the extremes of the excessive self-control of an ascetic and the insatiable search for instant gratification, there is a middle ground where a balanced enjoyment is possible: with pleasures that do us no harm. The anhedonic philosophy (the opposite of hedonism) is the obsession with emotional paralysis and the rejection of pleasure, as if it were counterproductive per se.

If you immerse yourself in a lifestyle that is miserly toward yourself, you will miss the opportunity to live passionately; it is impossible to learn to love yourself if you do not accept living intensely. Some people confuse "not feeling bad" with "feeling good." But not punishing yourself is not enough, you have to take one more step: reward yourself without excuses.

Why aren't we hedonists? Why do we settle for a routine lifestyle, void of pleasure? Maybe wanting to be "too human" has led us to lose some of the fundamental capacities that we inherited from our animal ancestors. The development of the cerebral cortex and language have allowed us to evolve in many aspects, but they have distanced us from the "primitive/instinctive" legacy of our evolutionary past, at least in two main ways: explorative behavior and the ability to feel. Let's look at each one in detail.

Explorative Behavior

Exploration is one of the behaviors that most guarantees the intelligent and emotional development of our species. In the animal kingdom, exploration and investigation of surroundings facilitates the discovery of food sources, shelters, and sexual mates. This natural impulse to investigate that moves individual beings helps the inherited behavioral system to be enriched and increases the resources at hand to face dangers and prevent them. It is a form of stimulation that develops more white matter in the brain (myelination) so that we can learn more, and in a better way. Exploring is being curious, and curiosity is one of the factors that has allowed for evolution and sustained life on the planet. Sniffing around, searching, and investigating all lead to one of life's greatest satisfactions: discovery and surprise. Exploring, delving into life, and being absorbed by it opens doors that were previously shut to your senses and knowledge, and allows you to collide with an unexpected reality.

Happiness doesn't just come knocking at your door, you have to look for it and fight for it every day. When was the last time you went outside to wander aimlessly or just improvised? When I push my patients to increase their motivational surroundings, many say to me, "And what do I do?" I tell them, "Search." Search for what? I have no idea! Look for looking's sake! An open, unguarded mind allows experiences and information to reach and pass through us. There is no predetermined list of what good things to do with our own lives, we have to write it ourselves by investigating and feeling our way around the environment that surrounds us: for every ten doors that you open, perhaps one will show you something interesting and wonderful that will justify the effort. When the everyday becomes too ordinary and you can predict your immediate future down to the last detail, something is wrong: it's time to worry because obsession is at play.

In other words, when run-of-the-mill becomes your ritual, it's time to explore. The more predictable your life, the more bored you will be. You need to get less used to your surroundings and build your own ecosystem, a motivating environment that inspires you to become a detective in your own life. If you have lost the ability to explore, you need to get it back; otherwise you will never be able to get close to a hedonistic philosophy, and self-love will be a burden.

The Ability to Feel: "I feel, therefore I am"

The second factor that interferes with a pleasurable lifestyle is roadblocks in the ability to feel. Some people only notice the obvious. For example, if they are at Niagara Falls, they will just see "tons of water," or when looking at a beautiful, medieval stained-glass window, they will see little more than "some painted glass"; the sunset will just be a reminder that it's nearly bedtime, a sunny morning will get them ready for a hot day, and the rain will just push them to find shelter so that they don't get wet.

Our primary senses have undoubtedly suffered from a sort of dulling. Smell and taste no longer have the same adaptive importance for our species, but they are sources of pleasure if they are reactivated (can there be anything more impactful than "experiencing" the person you love with all your senses?).

The part of the brain responsible for processing sounds has become a specialist in decoding the spoken language, but it has lost the ability to detect and distinguish other "sounds" of nature. The human information processing system operates in two ways. One is voluntary and controlled, and the other is automatic and unconscious. The former depends on the more developed layers of the central nervous system (left hemisphere of the cerebral cortex) and processes logical information. The latter is built on the bases of older physiological systems (limbic system, right hemisphere, autonomous nervous system) and processes emotional information. Feelings, unlike thought processes, have some unique properties: they tend to be more automatic; they require less mental effort; they are unavoidable, complete, difficult to describe in words, hard to explain, and often hard to understand. It's worth pointing out that while both types of processing have distinct characteristics, they constantly interact and mix and, depending on the case, one of the systems will be dominant. It's almost impossible for humans to have pure emotions or logic that is totally free of emotion.

This brings us to an interesting conclusion: If our feelings can possess their own channel for recognition and translation, they can also be blocked or facilitated by the influence of our thoughts. For example, one common belief that stops us from being comfortable with our emotions is the following: "Expressing your emotions freely means making a fool out of yourself." This belief, deeply rooted in many cultures and social groups, sees the repression of emotional expression as an act of social propriety and moderation. The problem is that not crying, shouting, feeling bewildered, "jumping for joy," or roaring with laughter every now and again, without apprehension or composure, is the same as being half dead. The norm that promotes "never going outside of the right lines" makes emotional repression a virtue.

One of my patients was a successful executive with a very traditional way of thinking; I had to give him the bad news that his wife, whom he adored, no longer loved him, that she was going to leave him, and that she had been having an affair for five years. When he received this enormous blow, he simply furrowed his brow, gave a slight nod, sighed, and monotonously replied, "I must admit I feel a little uncomfortable," before loosening his tie. He didn't lose his composure, he didn't show so much as a grimace of despair, nor did he shed a single tear or show any outrage. He just controlled himself and gave a hint of understanding while his gaze and sweat said something else altogether. Ironically, one of the causes of the end of his marriage was precisely the difficulty he had expressing his feelings in a relaxed and open way. The idea of inhibiting our emotions at all costs, whether it's for fear of feeling or fear of what people might say, is a custom that over time leads to a sort of "emotional dyslexia," an emotional illiteracy, where we not only stop expressing our emotions, but also stop reading and understanding them.

I am not encouraging blind impulsiveness and the complete lack of control of speaking harshly, crying all the time, and laughing over nothing. What I do not share is the absurd idea that the frank and honest expression of feelings is somehow "primitive," uncivilized, improper, and inconvenient. Improper according to who? Inconvenient for who? The ability to feel life, in the widest sense of the word, is not an illness that we have to build an immunity to; it is physical and mental health. You can get carried away without limits when you make love (howl if you feel like it), fly away with your favorite music until five in the morning (without disturbing your neighbors), cry in front of Michelangelo's *La Pietà*, scream at a horror movie, kick your car because it left you stranded for the fifth time, heartily hug a friend, say "I love you" seventy times to the woman or man you love, clap like crazy at a concert, or feel longing when looking at the photo of a relative who is no longer here. You can feel whatever you want to feel, as long as you do not violate other people's rights, if it doesn't cause you harm, and if it makes you happy, even if some emotionally stunted people don't like it and call you out for it.

It is true that some emotions are unpleasant and appalling, we psychologists know that well, but even in the cases where we need to modify a negative pathological feeling, the first step is to accept and recognize its existence. If it truly is a source of suffering and unease, we have to let the emotion out in order to start eliminating or restructuring it. "Feeling" is not the masochistic attitude of simply accepting those emotions that harm you. "Feeling," as considered here, is a way of investigating and exploring what you like and dislike; it is the essential condition needed to discover new ways of loving yourself.

To sum up what has been said so far, accepting a life of hedonism is generating a personal style of emotional freedom. An uninhibited spirit, free from irrational restrictions, will be more beneficial to the development of sharp, perceptive sensibilities, which will in turn improve emotional communication and an understanding of internal states. A hedonistic lifestyle leads to greater sensitivity to natural stimuli that reach our organism and widen the range of potentially pleasurable situations.

In one of his poems, French poet Jacques Prévert gives an example of emotional freedom that, although it is sanctioned by "good manners," recalls the joy and freshness of our childhood. It's titled "The Dunce":

> *He says no with his head*
> *but he says yes with his heart*
> *he says yes to what he loves*
> *he says no to the teacher*
> *he stands*
> *he is questioned*
> *and all the problems are posed*
> *sudden mad laughter seizes him*
> *and he erases all*
> *the words and figures*
> *names and dates*
> *sentences and snares*
> *and despite the teacher's threats*
> *to the jeers of infant prodigies*
> *with chalk of every color*
> *on the blackboard of misfortune*
> *he draws the face of happiness.*

A Case of Emotional Restriction of Joy

Many people are so concerned about excesses that they do not even begin to enjoy things in small doses. I have met people who place conditions on everything, including delight and hilarity, because too much joy is scary (if you are too happy, it won't be long before you head to the psychiatrist with a sign saying you are suffering from hypomania or mania). Fear of losing control turns them into party poopers. A few years ago, I went to a five-year-old boy's birthday party in a beautiful cabin nestled in a woodland area far from noise and the city. Everything seemed to point to a wonderful afternoon, if it weren't for the nagging of the birthday boy's mother, who was anti-commotion and controlling. When the children's noise level exceeded the permitted decibels, and when they were running around too fast, she would raise both arms, step into the cyclone of children, and, like an orchestra conductor, try to encourage a new, much slower, and more measured rhythm. Her words had something of a hypnotic tone to them, "Easy, easy, easy… calm down… calm down…" This pacified the children for a few moments as they stopped to look at the woman, but after two or three seconds of stupor, the infant whirlwind returned to its natural impulses. After a few hours watching this back and forth, I decided to ask her, very politely, why she didn't just let the kids play freely. "After all," I said, "we are out in the countryside and they aren't bothering anyone. Also, it's your son's birthday…" With a chuckle, she answered, "Everything has its limit," to which I responded, "I agree, but it can be hard to place limits without going too far." She regurgitated from memory, "All extremes are bad," which gained approval from some of the guests. I felt strongly that the children could not enjoy themselves under her watch, but I stopped trying to convince her. Nevertheless, some cases defend themselves, and that is exactly what happened. Later, when she stopped for the umpteenth time to audit the fun, one of her son's guests looked at her angrily and shouted, "This is so stupid! Why did you invite us if you won't let us play?!" You could hear a pin drop. The woman managed an awkward smile and tried to sidestep the honesty of the mini-Spartacus by asking who wanted some more meat. She didn't bother them for the rest of the afternoon. Although I tried, I couldn't stop that deep feeling of satisfaction that was served to me on a silver platter.

Many of my patients, victims of an "anti-joy" education, take up the vice of not enjoying things too much. When they are feeling really good, a psychological obstacle blocks them from the climax and thrusts them into the jaws of monotony. They fear joy because they see it as too dangerous and worldly; much like in Umberto Eco's novel, *The Name of the Rose*, when the blind priest forbade the reading of humorous religious texts because he believed that if fear in God was lost, all faith would come to an end. Fortunately, despite the dogmatic, restrictive, and controlling efforts of the friends of sobriety and austerity, joy inevitably triumphs, just like that afternoon at the birthday party.

SELF-PRAISE

How we speak to ourselves plays an important part in the way we feel and act. We are constantly having internal dialogues and chewing over this or that, consciously or subconsciously, simply because the mind is a compulsive chatterbox. These conversations the "self" has with itself start at a very young age and, over the years, they begin to form a sort of "internal language," which can be beneficial or harmful to our life, depending on its content. It is impossible to maintain prolonged inner silence, unless you are an advanced meditator. You will always have something to say to yourself, good or bad, constructive or destructive, enriching or depressing.

When we talk about self-praise, we are referring to a positive and/or constructive way of speaking to and congratulating ourselves when we believe we have done well. You don't need to do it out loud and in public—there would be disapproval and you would be harshly criticized—but you can whisper it (nobody will know and it will be hidden flattery "from you to you"). Self-praise (e.g., "I did such a great job!", I was awesome!", "I like the way I am") tends to be just as important for our self-esteem as external reinforcement, or perhaps even more so. The advantage with this is that you don't need any middlemen: you can be your very own Cyrano de Bergerac and whisper sweet nothings in your own ears.

Three Irrational Beliefs that Stop Us From Congratulating Ourselves

While there can be many causes, there are three main factors that we need to consider when explaining why our internal dialogue is not self-reinforcing:

a. *"I don't deserve it" or "It wasn't a big deal."*
   This is typical of those who see modesty, albeit fake, and undervaluing personal achievements, as an act of virtue. In most cases, it's actually an act of hypocrisy because when we act correctly, we know that we did well, we know that it was the result of effort, skill, or ability. A wise man does not deny his virtues, he simply doesn't go out in search of approval and plaudits; but he does not kid himself. If you are good at something, what are you going to do? Accept it and accept yourself! If the members of your community pay you honest and frank recognition, don't downplay it or make them believe that they were wrong. Don't say you do not deserve it. Say

thanks and keep quiet! This also refers to people who have such unattainable goals that praise and congratulations never materialize. Their irrational belief is as follows: "No congratulations are worth that much." If that sounds like you, try to relax. You don't need to win a Nobel Prize or carry out Herculean endeavors to give yourself positive reinforcement. You are always worthy of your own praise, if it is authentic and done for the right reasons. You aren't a hero, you are just a survivor, a person who lives, or at least tries to do it, well. Shouldn't that be enough to like yourself?

b. *"It was my duty" or "It was an obligation."*
This attitude is no good for your self-esteem. Did you carry out your duty well? Be happy! Give yourself a pat on the back! Your first duty is to yourself. Give yourself a hug! Even in the most authoritarian and strict systems praise and rewards are given. If your inner monologue is that of absolute obligation, you will not feel you have the right to praise yourself. You will see that as an act of cowardice and cast aside the pleasure of giving yourself any symbolic medals.

c. *"Praising yourself is tasteless."*
As I said previously, if you do this within your own internal jurisdiction, nobody will even notice. Self-praise is a necessity that goes alongside self-pres-

ervation. Your mind becomes more secure and powerful when you pamper it. Is it in poor taste to fart, urinate, snore, or yawn? Most likely, if you do it in public, but when you are on your own, you can allow yourself to do these and many other things. Self-praise, by definition, is an act that is carried out alone, without spectators of any kind; it's just for you. Cultivating healthy self-love (self-care) is never tasteless. On the other hand, punishment is, because it is an attack on human dignity and self-respect. Is it feeding the ego? That depends on how you do it. For example, you can carry out physical exercise to "improve your health" or to get into the "great body club." You can study a lot to gain knowledge or to beat your classmates. You can praise yourself to care for your mind and strengthen your "self" or to cultivate your narcissism. You decide.

External Praise that Can Become Self-Praise

The same praise that we direct at others can be applied to ourselves. The following classifications might help you to better understand how praise works:

a. *Impersonal praise*
   Widely encouraged by the culture of good manners and etiquette, this is considered to be a sign of proper education and diplomacy. In these cas-

es, what is being admired are material possessions, making no mention of any personal characteristics and without involving the person in the compliment: "Your shirt is very nice," "You have a lovely home," or "Your perfume smells great." The receiver generally accepts the compliment of their material object with a "thank you." This can hardly be considered an expression of feelings or affection, it is more an act of politeness, whether it is genuine or not. In any case, you should at least try to be polite with yourself, complimenting the material things that you genuinely like. Congratulate yourself for having them!

b. *Personal praise*

This partially involves the person the praise is directed at. Some people dare to go one step further when expressing what they feel and, as well as referring to the object, they tangentially mention the person: "That shirt looks good on you," "That haircut suits you," or "Your house shows you have good taste." This type of praise is more demanding, but still requires little commitment from the person portraying the message. You can include yourself in your own self-praise: "This shirt looks good on me," "My house definitely shows that I have good taste," "This swimsuit suits me," "I'm very well dressed today," "I'm really good at choosing my friends," and so on.

c. *Praise aimed at certain personal characteristics*
   This requires greater commitment from the compliment-giver: "You are very smart," "You have a beautiful body," "Your voice is incredible," "You are an amazing person," or "You are a good friend." As you can see, the praise is aimed at other people's characteristics, values, physical attributes, or abilities. Look for what you like about yourself, compliment yourself, and while you're at it, thank yourself just like anyone who received the compliment would thank you.

d. *Praise directed at the person, which also includes the praise-giver*
   Very few people are capable of giving this type of praise without feeling ridiculous, nervous, or insecure, unless they are very close to the person they are giving it to. Here, the praise-giver explains what the person inspires in them. A feeling is associated with the compliment: "I admire your intelligence," "I love your body," "I adore your smile," or "I envy your joyfulness." Expressions of affection aimed at other people have so many conditions and requirements in our culture that it is harder and harder to say "I love you" to someone without them suspecting some ulterior motive. The free and frank expression of positive feelings for those around us is not easy if our culture is not expressive. However, these issues of social inconformity do not exist when it comes

to complimenting your own characteristics. Saying to yourself, "I like my eyes," "I love being smart," "I really like my legs," or "I am a good person," has no risk associated with it and cannot be misunderstood; it's all about you.

The conclusion is evident: Expressing positive feelings toward ourselves makes us feel good, simply because being treated well is pleasant.

How to Praise Yourself

The most important step is to connect to a controlled process; in other words, to become aware of your inner monologue and what you say to yourself. You might discover that you don't say anything to yourself (your success has gone unnoticed) or that you punish yourself (your success has been insufficient for your aspirations): "I should have done better". I recall that when I was twenty, the academic demands I placed on myself reached absurd levels. At the time I was studying electronic engineering, a degree I quit when I decided to be honest with myself. The point is that despite my lack of calling for cables and chips, I would become deeply depressed if my grades slipped below 90 or 100. While my classmates celebrated a 70 in algebra, I would punish myself (verbally) for an 80. The dissatisfaction with my own performance could not accommodate any self-praise, because in my rigid view, it was crazy to think that a 60 or 70 deserved so much celebration. Now I know the undeniable fact that I can congratulate myself for whatever I want, because each of us sets our own standards. The excessive demands on myself were harmful to my mental health: they didn't just cause stress, but also sadness and dissatisfaction.

The following method will help you to acquire the healthy habit of self-praise:

a. As I've mentioned, the first step involves becoming aware of how you treat yourself and what you say to yourself. You can do this by keeping a detailed record for one or two weeks, which focuses on the behavior that is susceptible to self-praise and what you say to yourself once you carry it out.

b. The second step is to take stock, without notes or records now, of whether or not you praise yourself when you do something well. In the initial stages, self-praise should be done out loud (when alone) so that you can hear yourself: "That was good!", "Great job!", etc.

c. The third step involves giving yourself praise quietly, until it becomes a thought or internal language. Speak to yourself silently, think well of yourself and say it out loud, whisper it to yourself.

d. The fourth step is to try it regularly, so that it is reinforced through practice and becomes automatic, just as we learn to drive a car or type. Remember this: self-praise, like any reinforcement method, should be used discriminately, it should be selective so that it doesn't wear out and lose its power. You can choose which behavior is worthy of your self-praise, but if you want to maintain its motivational ability, don't use it blindly or compulsively. Don't waste it. Praising yourself when you think it's worth it is a special present to yourself. It isn't a gift to give yourself for the sake of it, but something that you believe you deserve.

A Self-Praise Summary

You possess the innate ability to speak to and understand yourself. This inner monologue, to which only you are privy, has an enormous influence on the way you act and feel.

> These verbal statements aimed at yourself have the power to make you feel good (via flattery, praise, and respectful treatment) or bad (through punishment, mocking, contempt, and disrespect). When you say to yourself, "I am capable, so I should trust myself," you are praising your-

self. If you say, "I'm the most ridiculous human on the planet," you are disrespecting yourself and treating yourself badly.
- ➢ If the self-praise follows positive behavior, this behavior will be reinforced and will be more likely to repeat in the future. Apply this to all behavior that you believe is worthwhile and that makes you grow as a human being.
- ➢ Do not praise yourself for bad things or behaviors that are not kind; this will only feed the base negative structure. Praising yourself for hurting someone, getting a bad grade, or betraying a friend does not make you better, it makes you worse.
- ➢ Finally, self-praise has its own advantages: it is quick, cheap, can be applied wherever and whenever, it is not seen (but it is felt), others cannot criticize it, it is exclusively for personal use, and, if used carefully, it does not run out.

TREATING AND REWARDING YOURSELF

This is another way of showing yourself affection. Rewarding ourselves is the process by which we self-administer positive incentives (things or the possibility of an activity) that we like and make us feel better. Although it might seem strange, something so obvious, so intrinsic to being human, becomes lost and tangled for many people.

One of my patients, an elderly gentleman who suffered from moderate depression, hated being in his house and he didn't know why. His common complaint was, "I walk into my house and I get depressed, I become irritable, it puts me in a bad mood!" Eventually, I decided to personally go to this man's home to find out why he was so uncomfortable there. My exploration led me to discover several reasons—some seemingly unimportant—that really did not help with the man's well-being. Many of them had inexplicably been in his environment for years, coexisting as inevitable negative designs, seemingly impossible to eliminate. For example, on the dining room's main wall, next to the table, hung an enormous painting of four terrified, rampant horses in a great storm, reminiscent of the Apocalypse. His bedside table's drawer (where he kept his glasses, medicines, etc.) was askew and almost always fell to the floor when he tried to open it. The bedroom walls were painted a penetrating mustard color (which he said he couldn't stand). Most of the towels that he used were matted and starchy ("I need to buy some towels," he would constantly promise himself); his bedsheets were too short and his feet would get cold in the middle of the night; he hated the layer of skin that formed on milk but his strainers let it through; the curtains in the library did not block out enough light, making it difficult for him to read; the small radio that connected him to the world had problems with the sound. And the list went on. The most surprising thing is that the man had the money and resources to change these things, but he didn't. He had grown used to suffering the small and unbearable discomforts of his surroundings or, in other words, he had lost the ability of self-reinforcement. We all have a bit of that old patient within us and sometimes we get so caught up in suffering that we start to see it as our natural state. And I'm not talking about horrible, uncontrollable pain, but simple, day-to-day issues that could be resolved in a heartbeat.

Some people accept living with things they don't want or that cause them displeasure simply because they feel guilty about getting rid of them. I bet your closet is filled with plenty of clothes you don't like or wear, but they're still there: shoes that have gone out of style, jackets from when you were two sizes smaller, faded shirts, and other such apparel. We all suffer a little from what is known as Diogenes syndrome, and we hoard useless and absurd items (maybe we're waiting for World War III or something). A friend of mine with this habit still carefully stores away stained tablecloths and a horrendous set of dishes she was given on her wedding day that she has never used or will ever use. Her bed creaks so much that she wakes herself up each time she moves. The argument she puts forward for not tossing the bed as far away as possible is "It's not that bad… I can bear it…" Our life shouldn't be "not that bad," we should be living our best life possible! It's not a question of emphasizing how horrifying or bearable it is, it's about our philosophy of life. And that brings us to our next point.

The Culture of Miserliness, or When Saving Becomes a Problem

Closely linked to Diogenes syndrome is the obsession with saving. This unchained and obsessive love for saving at all costs makes us keep a plethora of useless objects. If you accumulate too much, you will end up living like a pauper and being buried like a king. I am not defending neglect and irresponsibility with personal property; the idea is not to live a few years of opulence and the rest of your life in absolute misery. The saving spirit is good if used wisely and in moderation, and without turning it into an end in itself; it's a long-term attitude. Having for the sake of having puts you on the side of the miserly, while spending for the sake of spending puts you on the side of the spendthrift. I know people who are incredibly meticulous about saving money, collecting it like stamps.

Often, even though we have the resources, we doubt whether we should treat ourselves. One of my patients really loved strawberries and cream, but every time they bought a serving, they were left wanting more. Inexplicably, they never ordered two servings, or even three or four. When I suggested that they treat themselves, they really enjoyed the homework. I remember them asking me, "Can I really do that?" Why? Fear of excess. Another man with severe self-esteem issues would bring very special olives from Italy and wanted to eat them. But each time he opened the cupboard and saw the beautiful, large jars filled with black olives, he'd restrain himself. The problem stemmed from the fact that every time he suggested to his wife that they eat them, she would give him a strange look because she didn't consider it to be a "special occasion that merited trying them" (they were expensive and a limited edition). In a session, noting his concern, I suggested he break his habits (and those of his wife), take one of the jars, and eat it with the greatest pleasure possible, savoring them one by one, with no guilt or remorse, like a naughty child breaking a rule. I remember the man looking at me filled with happiness, as if I had given him permission, and saying, "Thank you, thank you!" When his wife lashed out at him for eating two entire jars on his own, the man responded, "It was the doctor's orders." The bottom line is this: If you prefer to spend your money at drugstores and on psychologists and doctors, don't indulge, restrain yourself.

The stingy philosophy of those who are too attached to money and material things does not allow for self-reinforcement. A cheapskate will always see the reward as unnecessary, as said reward does not produce anything tangible. They will say, "It's not necessary, or vital, or life and death." What is the benefit? Pleasure, pure pleasure.

You Are Not the Exception: You Need to Reward Yourself

You need to reward yourself with things and activities. Just like self-praise, self-reward builds up your self-esteem and does not allow self-punishment and dissatisfaction to prosper in your life. It's useless to take a hard line and be totally insensitive, as if you were a Stoic in a different time. A lack of self-reinforcement will not make you more psychologically robust or harden you; it will make you unhappy. When you have done something worthwhile or simply because you feel like it, treat yourself. Every now and again, indulge in a loving act toward yourself.

Take a moment to think about some cravings that you might have had in the past. Think carefully about how many of them you didn't indulge in simply because you decided not to. It's actually not because you couldn't, but because you didn't bring yourself to do it. You didn't have the courage to go off course and step outside the impassive, thrifty, and contemplative attitude of a person who leaves for tomorrow what they should do today. Food, clothes, jewelry, or other material things are not the only ways of self-reinforcement. Treating yourself implies the self-administration of anything that makes you feel good and that is obviously not harmful to your health, to others, or to the world you live in. Participating in activities that you like, or no longer doing something unpleasant, is another way to reward yourself. Honestly ask yourself these three questions: How often do you reward and treat yourself? How much time do you dedicate to yourself each week? Have you built a pleasant motivational space around you?

Anyone who knows how to love themselves leaves their mark on everything. Their territory is "designed" for and by them. Start with the basics: look at some aspects of your environment and try to remodel what you do not like. For example, think about your house, your social life, and your leisure activities. Is your home adapted to your needs? How many things bother you yet remain with you? What would you like to do with your bedroom? How many "friends" aren't really friends, but they are still around playing that role? How many places do you end up at that you don't really want to go to? How many foods do you eat that you actually hate when you could eat something else? Do you plan fun activities? How long has it been since you have gone to places you like simply because "there isn't time" or "it's not the right time"? In short, ask yourself if what you have built around you contributes to your happiness or if it buries you alive. A lot of people will say that it is hard, that the twenty-first century compels us to move too fast, and we're constantly buried in stress, consumerism, and crises. All the more reason to "seek refuge" in a lifestyle that balances the adrenaline rush and provides immunity with pleasure, however simple and mundane it may seem. You don't need to be a millionaire to do it! Self-rewards will help you, and they are in your hands. Go for it.

Stop Worshipping Repression

As we've seen so far, self-esteem can be strengthened in a number of ways. These paths to growth have been influenced by social learning, and they are often blocked by certain irrational beliefs. We have created a sort of devotion to a collection of traits that we consider synonymous to being "good people." We have grown to believe that these typically human attributes dignify and elevate us; they place us above other living species and allow us to go about our lives in a more dignified manner.

Despite the good intentions of our ancestors, and without denying that such virtues exist, some of these ideas have been taken to extremes that are harmful to our own self-esteem and sensitivity. These ritualistic ideas include worshipping habituation, rationalization, self-control, and modesty. These can become enemies of your self-esteem. Sooner or later, the disproportionate exaltation of these four beliefs will lead us to personal contempt and underestimation. If you follow them to a tee, you will become a "stable" person who is adapted to their environment and the expectations placed on them by society and proper manners. But something "stable" can also be immobile, unchanging, unfeeling, impassive, definitive, and constant. A bit like a tree or a granite monument. The indiscriminate use of these beliefs will only lead to the "ignorance" of feelings and the inability to express what you think and feel.

> ➢ Worshipping habituation will stop you from innovating and discovering new worlds. Change in any sense will be impossible and you will invariably be left behind. The universe will be reduced to a collection of behaviors, all predictable and preestablished. Habituating is becoming used to something, losing your sensitivity, becoming hardened. Forming calluses is useful sometimes, in combat for example, when a fighting spirit and bravery is required or when you have to adapt to complex situations, but turning it into a lifestyle means negating yourself as a person. You will confuse the old with the new, you will head north when you want to go south. How can you reward yourself if you have lost sensitivity and the ability to be amazed?
> ➢ Worshipping rationalization will turn you into a sort of walking computer. You will filter absolutely all feelings in order to evaluate them and decide whether they are convenient, suitable, or justified. This procedure will help you avoid bad emotions and keep them at a distance, but if you overdo it and try to explain what you shouldn't

and can't explain, you will distort pleasant emotions. There are moments when questions are unnecessary. Why do you like vanilla or chocolate ice cream? You most likely have no idea, and the smartest thing would be not to delve into it, unless you want to turn the experience of savoring a delicious ice cream into an existential problem. Romantic feelings will become a chess match or a problem that needs to be solved; the sexual act will turn into the juxtaposition of two reproductive organs; a beautiful sunrise or sunset will be seen as the rotation of the Earth around the sun; and so on. Not everything requires a rational explanation, just as not everything needs to be met with the dramatic sentimentality of a soap opera. I love my daughters because I love them, not because they are good, pretty, or intelligent. It's love, period. The last thing I want to do with that love is question it. Poorly placed questioning can block full, structured perception. Some things are not meant for pondering, they are just there to vibrate with (as long as they're not harmful to you or anybody else). How can you reward yourself if everything has to go through methodic doubt and a lack of spontaneity?

➤ Worshipping self-control is a roadblock to all your feelings and emotions. You will fear excess so much that you will forget to feel and enjoy; little by little, you will become an emotional statue. As I said before, moderate, well-placed self-control is vital to resisting several destructive temptations; however, the key to not straying too far from happiness is avoiding the "absolute containment" that some people preach. Do you never cry? Well then, you need help. Do you never lose control? You are either an enlightened lama or a repressed person on the edge of a nervous breakdown. Do you never let tenderness blossom? Then you should go see a therapist. How does your partner know that you love them? Do they infer it or do you show it? Do you laugh at the top of your voice or is the best you can muster a smile? You need help. Life is an inner battle between the "I want," "I should," and "I shouldn't," and true wisdom lies in maintaining the necessary balance to know when to take your foot off the brakes and when to apply them, when to give in and when to stay true to your principles. Again, I am not saying that having absolutely no self-control is the best way forward, but I am equally worried about trying to maintain 100 percent self-control all the time, as perfectionists and rigid minds try to do. Indifference and generally letting things happen will make you vulnerable to any addiction; worshipping self-control will not let you breathe, it will stifle your life. How can you reward yourself if you are living within yourself and if you see suffering as

something to bear (or even wear with pride) and not eliminate?
- ➤ Worshipping modesty will lead to you not valuing your successes and efforts. I'm not talking about bragging about your achievements, boasting to others, and parading around with them shamelessly. But if you hide your strengths in a bid for approval, you are doubly irrational: you are denying your good side and craving the approval of others in order to function. Are you actually ashamed of your strengths and virtues? Humility has nothing to do with feelings of worthlessness or low self-esteem: a humble person respects themselves just the right amount. Virtue is not ignorance of oneself. If extreme modesty is interiorized and embedded in the mind as an alleged value, it will be hard to let our abilities progress positively. Some people even feel guilty or uncomfortable if they are very good at something and they develop what is known as "false modesty," which is worse, because it implies lying about oneself. Without vanity or narcissism, let your virtues follow their course: don't hide them, enjoy them, make the most of them, follow them with passion, even if they are noticed. How can you reward yourself if you hide your values?

Allow your traditional values to make room for some changes, allow your modesty to slip a bit of self-praise, allow your reason to let emotions come out to play every now and again, allow your self-control to permit a slip-up, and allow yourself to go off budget sometimes. Give yourself the freedom and the space to move. Allow yourself permission to act. These are all good permissions.

To stop worshipping these traits means to recognize that some values, if taken too far, can affect self-esteem and make you more prone to countless disorders. It means that it is not advisable to take the previously mentioned beliefs to heart or turn them into indisputable tenets; such a dogmatic view will make you feel like a sinner every time you don't follow them word for word. You will feel guilty for loving yourself or for being happy.

IMPROVING YOUR SELF-REINFORCEMENT

The following action plan can help you move closer to a lifestyle that allows you to build yourself up or reward yourself with determination and joy.

1. Make Time for Pleasure

Life is made for more than just work. We work to live, not vice versa. Your relaxation time, your leisure, and your vacations are not a "waste of time," but an investment in your mental health. Don't put off satisfaction waiting for the "right day": there is no schedule for love, just like there is no schedule for loving yourself; you can define it according to your needs. Don't turn responsibility into an exhausting and dogmatic obligation, don't irrationally drown in it. There are moments for prudent and timely obligation, and others when the meaningless "musts," rules, and demands are not needed. Don't be afraid of pleasure: your joy is the joy of the universe, as the mystics say. God has a good time when you have a good time.

2. Decide to Live Hedonistically

Accept that the search for pleasure is a human condition. Being a hedonist is not promoting idleness, irresponsibility, or vices that go against your health; it is living intensely, exercising your right to feel good, and making the most out of every pleasant moment. It would be an inhumane act against yourself to deny this possibility. Take a moment to think about what truly motivates you, what you like and do not like, and whether in the monotony of your day-to-day life, you have forgotten to connect to your positive emotions. Think back on the times that you have unnecessarily and irrationally avoided seeking pleasure due to the belief that it was not the right thing to do or for fear of excess. Or, worse still, how many moments of happiness have you lost because you believed you didn't deserve them? Seek the forgotten passion inside you, the one that never goes out and insists that you do what you want. If you empower your pleasurable experiences, new doors will open for you and you will become immune to the worst disease of all: boredom.

3. Don't Rationalize Pleasant Emotions So Much

The idea here is not to deny the importance of thought; in fact, the way you think has a direct impact on your feelings. The problem is that when you try to "explain yourself" and constantly understand your feelings, you inevitably obstruct them. You block their flow, you inhibit them, you distort them and impede their proper development.

Take a walk one day with the simple goal of listening to the sounds of where you live. You will hear a bunch of things: rustling, far-off voices, the clicking of planks rocked by the wind, a distant car, a bird, the breeze. An understandable language that goes unnoticed by a mind that is an expert in the spoken language. On your daily walks, take a detailed look at the things around you: a poster, a door, the faded colors of the sidewalks, a bush, people's faces, the natural comings and goings of the world you belong to. You are in it! When you observe it, don't be an evaluating inquisitor, just gaze at it and let yourself be carried away.

If you sit down to eat, enjoy your food as if you were an unnamed and experienced critic giving it your full backing: focus on the flavor, just the flavor. Take a bit longer to taste the food; savor it and leave it in your mouth until your tastebuds take it in completely. Eating is not simply chewing and swallowing! Don't eat just to avoid dying of starvation; relish it and stimulate your sense of taste, dive into it, feel it from within. You don't need a banquet; any food, however simple, can be turned into a delicacy.

Equally, lower your resistance thresholds and get back your sense of smell. Smelling isn't rude; and I am not just referring to sniffing a good wine or designer perfume, but rather to everything that is worth a smell, such as food (even if people might say that is unseemly), flowers, hair, the breeze, horses, the sunrise, smoke, new things, plastic, clean things, dirty things. Smell is one of the main tools for sensual pleasure-seekers. The entire universe is sensual, everything enters through your senses, everything explodes before you so that you can grasp it through the channel of your choosing.

Finally, your entire body has the ability to feel through touch. Your skin is the greatest sensor. Unfortunately, due to its relation to human sexual activity and the attitude held by many religions, this has historically been the most punished and censored of the senses. Don't fear your skin, it will put you in contact with a world that has been numbed by the use of clothes, by shame and taboos. It will allow you to establish more direct and often more impactful contact than that which is produced by seeing or hearing, given that its structure is more primitive and intense (nobody can hug you at a distance, as much as the internet tries). The sense of touch does not only allow you to "touch" a person, a smooth or rough surface, something cold or hot, it also allows you to be "touched" by another human being or any object. Your skin doesn't have some "offensive or vulgar meaning," as some prudes would have you believe (they also like touching and being touched, even if it pains them to admit it). When you caress someone, concentrate on the feeling, on the sensation, on the direct connection; let yourself be taken away by the "chemistry," by each membrane and pore that opens up and responds wonderfully to the stimulus. Play with your fingers slowly, slide them, rest them, remove them; this is physiologically enchanting. Walk barefoot, roll around in the grass, hug a lonely tree, and then, when you take a shower, do not dry off immediately, just spend a while observing how the water evaporates off your skin, feel it running off you slowly. Go out to walk in the rain, without an umbrella or a fixed destination; look for something you have never touched and touch it. Physical contact is the best way to communicate emotions; you don't need to talk or justify or elaborate or explain anything. Everything you need to say is expressed when you genuinely do this.

4. Activate Self-Praise and Put It to Work

Do you fear congratulating yourself? Does it feel arrogant or childish? Or maybe you think you don't deserve it? Well, if you don't do it, you are neglecting yourself psychologically. Self-care is more than just going to the doctor for your yearly checkup. We all deserve support, no matter where it comes from; rewarding yourself lifts your spirit and encourages the organism to continue living better. When you manage to achieve something that was difficult for you or if you dared to overcome a fear that incapacitated you or to face a situation where you felt insecure, don't act as if nothing has happened! Embrace yourself, give yourself a kiss, and recognize yourself as the main player in your achievement! Whisper something rewarding in your ear: "Good job! You did it!" or "I have been brave!" or "You were great!" Don't be afraid, justified self-praise when deserved will not turn you into an unbearable narcissist; it will simply make you a stronger and more secure person; it will help you work better with yourself. If you don't congratulate yourself when you do something worthwhile or when you reach a vital goal, your "self" will feel dejected. Does that sound odd to you? Well, it's not. It happens on a daily basis. There are people who hate themselves, who can't stand themselves, who self-sabotage, who live in discord with who they are, who have no confidence in themselves, just as might happen in any interpersonal relationship. Self-praising establishes a good interpersonal relationship. You have to decide between your own self being at odds with itself (inner battle) or your own self being friends with itself (inner peace). Without a doubt, congratulate yourself until you no longer can! Make up with yourself!

5. Be Modest, But Don't Overdo It

Don't hide your attributes or reject them ("Sorry, I'm smart," "I didn't mean to offend you with my achievements"). It is not your fault if you possess some virtue or strength that helps you be successful in some aspect of life (not in terms of medals or great awards, but more like those day-to-day mini-wins that give meaning to existence but go unnoticed). In any case, what alternative is there? Losing on purpose? Hiding behind the curtain of false modesty? Denying yourself? Remember that modesty and humility do not mean negating or undervaluing your talents, but rather making them yours, without identifying yourself through them or becoming attached to them or seeking plaudits. Enjoy the natural talent that defines you, whatever it may be. Make a list of all the psychological and physical things you like about yourself and stick it somewhere in your house, in your car, at the office. Don't forget who you are. You cannot hide yourself from yourself. Heraclitus and other wise men throughout the ages have held that one must remain as anonymous as possible, but they didn't mean that you should be ignorant of your own qualities. Anonymous to spectacle, to social approval. Anonymous so that siren song does not whisper sweet nothings in your ears and inflate your ego. But when you are face-to-face with your essence, you have nothing to hide.

6. *Treat Yourself*

I know people who treat themselves, and then feel so guilty that they put themselves through suffering for a while to make up for the "sin" of self-reinforcement. They go into crisis mode for feeling good! I don't mean to suggest we should become pleasure addicts and spend money we don't have or do things we shouldn't do. I simply mean we should surround ourselves with things that we really want. People who are stingy with themselves tend also to be stingy with other people, and so they live bitter lives. Treat yourself whenever you can (and however you can) but be sure to do it. Don't wait for Christmas to give yourself or those you love a gift. If you are walking by a produce store and you see some beautiful, sumptuous apples and you know that your wife or husband likes them, why wait until it's the day you do the grocery shopping? Treat yourself by treating those you love. Give them a little present: their smile will be contagious.

And just in the same way that you have to make these gestures with others, you also have to give yourself a little present once in a while, and they don't necessarily have to be material things. For example: "Today I am going to give myself a half hour walk in the park," "Tomorrow I will visit a friend," or "I'm going to spend the whole day alone and in my pajamas." Treating yourself is being emotionally intelligent. I know somebody who feels strange and odd whenever she feels good, as if she weren't herself. She is so used to suffering that feeling good depersonalizes and distresses her, as if her "natural state" were pain. Treating yourself is the most basic and necessary self-care ritual.

7. Fight Against Psychological and Emotional Repression

Etch this into your mind: There can be no happiness if repression has made a home in your mind. Containment will make your life seem insignificant and remove the possibility of discovery and discovering yourself. Let go! Let your creativity, your heart, and your mind flow! If people do not like seeing you emotionally free, that is their problem. When was the last time you were spontaneous and truly expressive? Being repressed, overly controlling, self-critical, a perfectionist, formal, serious, harsh, rational, or stubbornly intellectual all the time is a syndrome, not a value. Have passion for life, make love to life. One of my patients has sex with his wife on the same days each month, in the same position, and in the same place. Too many "sames." Obviously, his orgasms and his wife's orgasms are always the same; repetitive, anticipated, boring. Even the greatest pleasure can lose its power if we become used to it and make it routine. "Repeating the repetition" ad nauseam and then resigning ourselves to it, that is the secret to unhappiness. A pinch of madness, an unplanned trip, an unexpected love, the poems we write without being poets, the cheek of sneezing at the top of our lungs in a library because the urge outweigh the rules; in short, being inoffensively out of your mind. I know that you are thinking "adults don't mess around." Lies! We do it mentally all the time. We fantasize, sublimate, and are bursting to run around aimlessly again, to have imaginary friends, to laugh until we explode. We envy children, their spontaneity, their incredible honesty, that is the truth. The good news is that your essence doesn't die; it sleeps, but it doesn't disappear. You just need to awaken it, stir the body and the soul, so that it can blossom and get back to doing its thing.

CHAPTER 5

DEVELOP STRONG SELF-EFFICACY

> *No one can make you feel inferior without your consent.*
> —Eleanor Roosevelt

As we saw in the first part of this book, we can mistreat our self-concept as a result of falling into the trap of setting irrationally high goals and having unrealistic ambitions. In other words, functioning with an overly competitive and self-critical style that is too strict with your own performance will lead to adaptive failure: the result will be an unstable and subdued self-concept.

However, expecting nothing of yourself is just as bad as expecting too much. The opposite extreme to those seeking success at all costs in order to feel fulfilled is occupied by those whose goals are hesitant, insecure, and minor, who stumble at the first hurdle and are indecisive when faced with problems. Just as placing excessive demands on oneself destroys and punishes self-esteem, a lack of ambition blocks psychological growth. It is just as bad to be obsessive as it is to throw in the towel too early. Challenges are the main sustenance for our self-concept and they even give meaning to life. If you don't have goals, if they are too easily attainable, or if you do not face your problems, your "self" will not be able to properly develop. Overheating the engine is just as bad as not even switching it on. Therefore, one of the biggest enemies of self-concept is a lack of trust in oneself, the fixation with creating failure scenarios, or believing that one is not capable. If you don't trust yourself, you won't be able to love yourself. The trust and conviction that it is possible to achieve your goals is known as self-efficacy. Low self-efficacy will lead you to believe you are not capable, while high self-efficacy will make you feel confident that you can reach your objectives, or at least fight for them. If you do not believe in yourself, you will enter a vicious cycle: Your personal challenges will be minimal, you will avoid facing your issues, and you will give up at the first obstacle that stands in your way, which will reinforce your weak self-efficacy ("I am not capable") and you will become less demanding of yourself. This downward spiral can continue to negatively affect you for years. Conversely, strong self-efficacy will make your goals more solid, allow you to persist in the face of unexpected hurdles and face problems in the right way; you will fight for what you believe in, persistently and self-assured, no matter what you gain.

Self-efficacy is basically an emotional opinion of oneself. Many people can think that they possess the necessary skills and abilities to obtain certain results and yet not be convinced that they will successfully reach their objectives. Let's consider an athlete about to do a pole vault jump with a gold medal on the line. Suppose that the competitor is sure they possess the necessary abilities for executing the jump successfully, they have trained well, they're in excellent physical shape, and have the crowd behind them. Let's also imagine that, in training, they had already beaten the height they are faced with. Everything in their favor. However, suddenly and inexplicably, they begin to doubt themselves. They ask themselves what we should never ask ourselves: "Will I be capable?" or "What if I mess up this jump?" If the doubt grows and sticks, it will generate anxiety and tension, their muscles will not respond, and the jump will not be a good one. And that will only be the beginning. Perhaps in their next competition they will anticipate failure due to a similar lack of confidence in themselves. The question will become a statement, "I am not capable," even if everything seems to be in their favor.

THREE CAUSES OF WEAK SELF-EFFICACY

The expectation to be successful does not solely imply, as one might think, a cold, rational analysis of the objective chances of success (expectations of results), but also the subjective assessment of how capable the subject feels (efficacy expectations). As with any belief, this appraisal is also a question of faith and trust. It is clear that mistrust in your own "self" can trounce the abilities and skills of any person. On a daily basis, in my psychological practice, I see people who possess all the necessary resources but fail because their self-efficacy is weak. Worse still, a considerable majority of them do not even fight for their goals; their argument is "I won't be able to do it, so why even try?" When I lay out the high probabilities of success, showing them that the pros outweigh the cons and that they have the necessary skills and intelligence, they tend to respond with "You're right… everything is on my side, but I don't trust myself." If I suggest they try anyway and take a risk just to see what happens, they stick to their dark prediction: "Why try if I know it's going to go badly?"

How do human beings reach the point where they doubt themselves and give in to suffering and adversity without even trying to generate change, even when they have the ability to do so? How do we generate such a "loser" self-schema? Why do we make negative predictions of our own performance in easy and potentially successful situations? Why do some people freeze up when faced with the chance to overcome difficulties that they are capable of overcoming? Although the answers vary, research in cognitive psychology indicates that at least three factors appear to be associated with low levels of trust in oneself: the perception that nothing can be done, the locus of control, and attributional styles. Let's look at each one in detail.

The Perception that Nothing Can Be Done

The impossibility of modifying a painful or stressful event causes depression and mistrust in oneself. If you are in a harmful situation and you think that nothing you do could possibly change it, that simple thought will reduce your strength and lead you to despair. For example, a history of successive failures might produce a perception of incapability and you will begin to consider success as very unlikely. The feeling of not having control ("nothing can be done about it") has a devastating effect on people's fight response, and even more so if they are not very resistant or resilient.

Let's consider a classic example from experimental psychology carried out a few years ago. Several small dogs were placed in a box with no escape and a floor made up of a grate connected to an electricity source. The experiment involved giving the animals unpredictable and inescapable electric shocks and observing their response. At the beginning, the dogs tried to escape. They jumped, barked, ran around the box, and so on. However, after a while, they began to show passive behavior: they remained still and isolated, looking sad and no longer eating, seemingly "resigned" to their own fate. The experiment team then decided to move them to a new box with a door added to it so that they could escape if they received shocks. The anticipated reaction to the new escape route was that the dogs would learn to avoid the electric shocks and leave through the door. But that didn't happen. To everyone's surprise, the animals continued to put up with the punishment and, despite repeated experiments, the dogs did not flee from the shocks. They ignored the new possibility of escape and resisted leaving. The only way for them to learn to avoid the electric shocks was to forcibly remove them from the box countless times in order for them to "understand" that the open door really was an opportunity for relief and a solution. The only therapy for the dogs was "showing" them the facts and repeatedly showing them that they were "wrong." The researchers concluded that this phenomenon, which they called learned helplessness, was caused by a perception in the dogs that "nothing could be done about it," given that the shocks were not controlled by them. In other words, the animals acted as if they had "perceived" that their efforts were futile and ineffectual in controlling the punishment and so they simply resigned themselves to the piercing pain. They thought that they had "done everything they could possibly do and nothing could save them." They could see the door, but not the escape route that it offered them.

Other experiments carried out on humans in situations where the subjects do not perceive that they have any control over the negative situations (not using electric shock) have produced similar results. The perception of not having control over adverse events produces a drop in self-efficacy or trust in oneself. A bad run tends to be enough to generate feelings of insecurity. Similarly, if failure is seen as unavoidable, feelings of inefficacy that can be generalized for new situations will come to the surface. The subject will come to consider themselves inept at finding almost any solution and, although they are presented with viable alternatives, sometimes right under their noses, they will discard them because they consider themselves incompetent.

Fortunately, as we will see in a bit, this discouraging panorama can be modified if you decide to dare to face your problems and take some risks. What you should never lose is your ability to fight. As Hermann Hesse said, "To achieve the possible, we must attempt the impossible again and again." While you are in the fight, there will always be hope that you can cling to; and if you lose and don't achieve what you had hoped, at least you tried. You won't feel like a coward, you won't feel guilty, and you won't start to suffer from avoidant personality disorder.

The Internal Locus of Control

Being subjected to uncontrollable and catastrophic events, such as earthquakes, floods, or war, is not the only cause of weak self-efficacy. Sometimes, not trying to modify harmful and unpleasant events is a result of culturally learned beliefs. Depending on where people determine their own behavior is controlled, they can either be considered "internally oriented" or "externally oriented."

- ➤ Individuals who have an internal locus place the control within themselves; they would say that they are the ones who guide their own behavior and they are largely responsible for what happens to them. They take responsibility for their destiny, not as something given from the outside, but as something they must build with their own effort and perseverance. Therefore, they do not tend to lay the blame for what happens in their life on others. In this sense, they are realists, they are determined, and they don't tend to accept defeat easily.
- ➤ On the other hand, externally oriented people believe that their behavior is affected by a swathe of events and causes outside of their control and which very little can be done about. For example, luck, the stars, UFOs, fate, and so on. They tend to be pessimistic and resigned to hardship. Their thinking causes paralysis: "Nothing can be done; it's just a question of fate," or "Why try?" If this belief becomes generalized, they will see any attempts to modify negative environments as unfruitful or a waste of time that will lead to nothing. Most of the time, using an external locus of control to act leads to weak self-efficacy.

The position that each of us takes in terms of what does and does not depend on us is largely determined by social learning and the models and value systems of our family and cultural groups. When it comes to faith or hope, the field of psychology suggests that if we act realistically or for personal growth (i.e., without denying our true self), these can be powerful sources of motivation. The phrase "God helps those who help themselves" is a great example of this point. Sitting around waiting for the universe to throw things onto our lap is not a good attitude. It is better to discern when to act according to an internal locus of control and when to let external factors carry you; in this regard, the middle ground is undoubtedly the healthiest option. Ancient wisdom is fairly spot on with this.

You are the one who writes your own story. God, the Universe, or Life has provided you with the ink and the paper, but you still have to write it. You have the power of thought and the gift of intelligence, not to make you a victim, but rather a victor. If you have the tendency to get carried away by an external locus of control, review the belief and make it more flexible and rational; if you believe in God, think of him as an adviser or a parent who respects his children's freedom; if you believe in astrology, remember that the stars often get it wrong—if your horoscope is "bad," challenge it. Things depend on you, more than you think, even if this can sometimes feel like a burden. And if you have faith in something or someone, let that be your motor and a source of conviction that you are capable of going about this world without too many crutches. Don't let that "faith" be the recliner you fall back on.

Attributional Styles

When we are faced with situations of success or failure, we humans make interpretations about the causes behind why each result came about. We try to understand what happened by seeking causal explanations of "how," "where," "when," and "why" certain things happened to us. Well, this ability to explain events can become a double-edged sword that, if used incorrectly, can negatively affect our self-efficacy. Let's take a look at an example of how a successful exam result can be interpreted differently by two teenagers who use opposing attributional styles.

Teenager One says: "I studied really hard. If I study like that all the time, I will do well in my other exams, and probably at college too."

Teenager Two says: "The exam was way too easy. I doubt the others will be like that. They are always harder."

Teen One attributed their success to themself, their own efforts and perseverance in their studies, concluding that their success will repeat itself in other exams and over time. Conclusion: their success was dependent on them. Teen Two attributed their success to external factors (the ease of the exam) and thought that future exams wouldn't be so easy or they wouldn't be so lucky. Conclusion: their success was not dependent on them, but on the exam's lack of difficulty. The first teenager was motivated to keep forging ahead and trusting themself, while the second did not trust their abilities. The first strengthened their self-efficacy. The second dealt a heavy blow to their self-esteem.

In situations of failure a similar thing could happen to you. If you say, "The failure was up to me, it will always be that way, in every situation," you will then feel incapable of taking on life. You will turn your future into a dark prophesy. But if you say, "The failure was only partly down to me, it doesn't always have to be like that," you will feel capable of giving it another try. You will turn your future into a hopeful prophesy. Loving yourself means recognizing your successes and not punishing yourself or putting yourself down for your failures but using them as a means of trying not to repeat them and learning.

Let's review and clarify. People who use a pessimistic and negative attributional style will feel responsible for their failures but not their successes. For their part, those who use rational, optimistic, and positive attributions will tend to evaluate situations objectively and take responsibility for their failures or successes in a constructive manner. The goal here is not to attribute what does not correspond to you and be irrationally optimistic or distort reality in your favor; it's not about taking credit for other people's successes and blaming your own failure on others. If you do that, your self-efficacy will not grow properly, it will inflate like a balloon until it bursts. Saving your self-efficacy and self-concept at the expense of others or denying the truth are not healthy solutions for your psychological integrity. Loving yourself in a healthy way means doing it in an honest way.

THE AVOIDANCE PROBLEM

One day, when I was ten, I went for a walk through my neighborhood with a neighbor I considered to be "my girlfriend," and I suppose she considered me "her boyfriend" too. When we got to a corner where a group of slightly older kids used to hang out, one of them lifted up my friend's skirt and stroked her behind. When I saw the size of my opponent and how his accomplices celebrated the feat, I simply chose to put my head down and keep walking next to her as if nothing had happened. The walk back seemed endless. When I got home, my father saw that I was clearly shaken up and asked me what had happened. When I explained, reproaching myself through my tears, he fixed his gaze on me and said, "Look, son, what just happened to you is extremely uncomfortable. Something similar also happened to me once. If you let fear beat you, it will take advantage of you." After pondering this a few seconds, I thanked him for his advice and headed toward the television. But I hadn't really understood. My father grabbed my arm and said firmly, "You didn't get me. You have two options: You either go out and face those idiots or you'll have me to deal with." Honestly, I didn't hesitate. My father was a Neapolitan immigrant from World War II who was to be feared when he saw red. So I opted for the more worthy, albeit forced, choice of salvaging my tarnished dignity. And that's what I did, I went back and I stood up to them. It goes without saying that the bruises and the black eye lasted several days. However, I should also admit that it was worth it. My girlfriend saw a real Prince Charming in me, I got credit among my friends, and other girls started showing an interest in my weird mix of Latin lover and little karate apprentice. But the most important result was the lesson the experience gave me in psychological terms. After the fight, my father was waiting for me with ice, aspirin, and a certain air of poorly hidden pride. "Well done," he said. "It's better to have a black eye than bruised dignity." That night I slept like never before.

Machiavelli said, "Ghosts are more frightening from afar than up close." That's true. The only way to overcome fear is to face it. Equally, the only way to solve a problem is to face it openly and with as little subterfuge as possible. However, despite the proven advantages of exposure therapy to treat what we fear, we humans avoid paying the cost of this self-improvement because it is uncomfortable. We opt for the easier path: the relief brought by avoidance and postponement. Avoidance blocks the organism from being exposed long enough to overcome fear, debunk the irrational beliefs that drive us to act unsuitably, or to solve problems we are faced with. Dealing with unpleasant things is annoying and can be painful, but that is the price of modifying and overcoming them. What would you think of someone who preferred not to cure their tonsillitis, knowing full well the serious consequences of a rheumatic fever, because they can't stand the sting of an injection?

In the most serious cases of panic disorders, it has been proven that the best therapeutic strategy is being exposed to the phobic source. In these cases, when the subject is exposed to fear, there is an adrenalin spike, and certain physiological reactions occur, including an increased heartbeat, sweating, temperature changes, nausea, dizziness, and so on. These sensations are uncomfortable, but if exposure is maintained for a sufficient amount of time, they become reduced, then disappear, and the organism becomes used to the feared object. This is known as fear extinction.

Unfortunately, we do not hold out for the necessary amount of time to become accustomed and we escape before extinction takes place. If you want to overcome your insecurities, you have to test yourself and expose yourself to them. You have to take a risk and contradict the unfounded or incorrect ideas you have of yourself. If you make avoidance a habit, you will never know how to value yourself.

Weak self-efficacy produces similar effects to those mentioned above. The feelings of insecurity produced by the idea that you are incapable stop you from holding out long enough to overcome any hindrances, as any obstacle will be seen as an impassable abyss that you have to get far away from as soon as possible. If you live like this, catastrophic predictions of absolute failure will never be countered and contradicted in practice.

Is the Danger Real?

Avoidance is not always inappropriate. There is no doubt that escape and avoidance are the best options when the danger—physical or psychological—is objective and genuinely harmful. Let's suppose somebody tells you that in the next room there is a hungry lion ready to knock the door down and then you immediately hear a thunderous, fearful roar. The lion, objectively, can cause you harm. If you sprint away from the furious animal, people will say, "That person sure is clever!" But if they tell you there is a little cat behind the door and, after stifling a scream and turning pale, you flee in fear, anybody who sees you running from the harmless little animal will say, "That person has a loose screw!" The cat, objectively, cannot do you any harm, even if you see it as the most ferocious predator. We psychologists call this kind of fear a phobia, an irrational fear, while the terror and subsequent escape from the lion is considered adaptive because it helps your personal survival and that of the species. The conditioning and learning responsible for avoidance have been very important for humanity. Many of our fears are "prepared" or inherited, because they served our prehistoric ancestors. Avoidance was (and is) a type of preemptive defense from potential predators. However, some people's danger "calculator" is far too sensitive, and they consequently see the world as incredibly threatening.

If you are faced with a situation that is difficult, but important or critical to you, ask yourself: "If I face this situation, are the consequences I'm afraid of real? Objectively, can something serious and irreparable happen to me? Is my calculator maybe exaggerating the consequences? Does what is at play justify this? Is the proposed goal attainable or not? Is there a probability of obtaining what I am looking for?" If nothing can objectively happen to you, don't hesitate, take the risk! If the probability of negative consequences is very high and there is nothing vital at play, consider it.

If you believe you are not capable and you feel sorry for yourself, grant yourself the opportunity to show yourself what you can do. The attempt might be uncomfortable at first; you will experience fear, pain, and unease, but something much greater than your physiological state will be at play: your self-esteem, your self-efficacy, what you think and feel about yourself. Self-respect and the dignity associated with it deserve the "sacrifice" of the initial needle prick. Face up to your fears, accepting that you have to pay the price of feeling bad for an instant; it's just an instant. Avoidance offers you immediate relief, but in the long-term it will end up reinforcing your feelings of insecurity and worthlessness. There is little doubt: a black eye is much better.

OVERCOMING WEAK SELF-EFFICACY

In summary, self-efficacy is the "cognitive/emotional opinion" that you have of the possibility of achieving certain results; in other words, the confidence you have that you can successfully reach your goals. As we have seen, the most common causes that contribute to weak self-efficacy are seeing things as out of your control, believing that your own behavior is regulated more by external factors than by yourself, and unfairly attributing responsibility of the bad in us and not the good in us and our personal achievements.

Any of these three factors produces a self-schema of mistrust and insecurity in oneself, which leads us to avoiding challenging situations, problems, or any event that implies a personal intervention for their solution. People will make avoidance a way of life. The following strategies will allow you to face weak self-efficacy or keep it at a suitable level.

1. Eliminate "I'm not capable" from Your Vocabulary

If you undervalue yourself, your inner monologue will act as a brake. Remove "I'm not capable" from your repertoire because each time you repeat it, you confirm and strengthen your feelings of insecurity. This negative evaluation will automatically stop you in your tracks. If the trainer of the previously mentioned athlete were to whisper in his ear just before a jump, "You are not capable," do you think the end result would be good? Many people have experienced first-hand the effects of a lack of confidence in family settings: "The boy isn't capable, it's best if you do it." How would you feel if, at work, your boss decided to give a special assignment to a colleague and said to you, "I gave the work to Juan because you aren't capable"? Even though you're not aware of it, the psychological consequences of telling yourself "I am not capable" are just as counterproductive as when other people say it to you. If you say, "I'm useless," "I'm a failure," "I'm an idiot," you will end up being one.

Every time you find yourself mulling over the awful "I'm not capable," get away from it and cast it out of your mind. Stop the thought by saying to yourself, "Stop!" "Enough!" Change what you are doing, make a phone call, listen to music, sing out loud, or guide your monologue in a positive direction, but don't let a negative thought drag another one in and for your mind to become a chain of self-destructive thoughts. For example, you can say to yourself, "This way of talking is not healthy for my mental health. Nobody is totally capable or incapable. In any case, I need to give myself another chance. Treating myself like this inhibits me, makes me insecure and doubtful. It's time to start respecting myself and treating myself well. If I put my mind to it, I will be capable."

2. Don't Be a Pessimist

People with a weak sense of self-efficacy anticipate the future in a negative manner and, when it comes to their own performance, their expectations are of failure and inability. They always see themselves as the worst actors in the movie. If you see failure coming in each of your actions, you won't even consider trying to remedy this. Negative prophesies tend to come true because we ensure they are fulfilled. For example, if you tell yourself, "It's going to go badly for me," the motivation, tenacity, and perseverance required to reach your goal will waver, you won't have enough energy, and your prediction will become a reality, through nobody's fault but your own! When you find yourself making lots of bad predictions about your future, ask yourself if you are being a realist or not. And once you've made your predictions, good or bad, make a habit of then verifying their validity; compare them with reality and see whether you were right or not.

This method of checking hypotheses against objective data will help you discover that your predictions don't tend to be so exact and that, over time, your skills as a soothsayer leave a lot to be desired. The habit of examining anticipated outcomes alongside reality will allow you to polish and perfect your deduction processes going forward.

Keep a detailed record of the right guesses and the errors. If some prediction does not come true two, three, or four times, discard it and do not use it anymore. For example, if you tell yourself "I'm terrible at conversation and girls or guys get bored with me," put that prediction to the test. Define exactly what you are expecting to happen: "They will make fun of me" (they will laugh, make gestures, and pull faces), "They will get bored" (they will yawn, want to leave quickly, and not speak), "They won't go out with me again," and so on. Use clear, defined categories that you can properly verify or refute. After going out several times with different people, you can compare what you were expecting with what really happened. If they didn't mock you, didn't seem bored with you, and if they went out with you again, your catastrophic predictions did not come true. And if they did come to fruition, you have a problem to resolve, with or without professional help, which isn't the end of the world because it can be fixed.

Put your predictions to the test, without cheating. Remember that a lot of the time we subconsciously do everything possible to self-sabotage and ensure that our prophecies come true. In a nutshell, try to develop within yourself the healthy habit of evaluating your capacity to make poor predictions. You will be pleased to find out how often you are wrong and what a bad clairvoyant you are.

3. Don't Be Fatalistic

You are the architect of your own future, even if that sounds trite and you don't like it (it's easier to trust that some angel will take care of you). At least you will agree that you largely shape your destiny. Therefore, you have the power to change a lot of things. Don't look at the world as unchangeable and perpetually immutable, governed by laws that stop you from altering the situations that make you uncomfortable. If you see an external locus of control for everything, you will tend to be pessimistic and see misfortunes as uncontrollable.

Remove the word "always" from your verbal repertoire. The past does not condemn you; in fact, the present is tomorrow's past, so if you change here and now, you will be contributing significantly to your destiny. It is true that events from your childhood and adolescent years have an influence on you, it would be absurd to deny that, but that influence is relative and can be modified (you aren't a small laboratory animal at the whims of the researchers). Humans, fortunately or unfortunately, are able to participate actively in constructing our story and restructuring the way we process information: we are not predestined for suffering.

If you place too much value on chance and luck, your self-efficacy will not be able to grow because you will see unscalable obstacles everywhere. When you make a cost-benefit analysis, include yourself as the main resource for tackling issues. The future is not just sitting there waiting for you to arrive, it's holding on for you to create it. On any random day you can make the decision to positively program yourself. For that day, imagine that you are the master of your life and the only judge of your own behavior. You can do and undo at your whim. That day you will be the musician and the conductor, and you will direct your steps with the firm conviction that you, and only you, are the craftsperson of what you want to achieve. Feel like the master of yourself, if only for one day. No horoscopes or external guides; you will be radically internal and challenge negative predictions, no matter where they come from. You will make your own prophecies and have a go at being a version of yourself that feels victorious. Try it out for one day. If you like it, you will keep trying, as there is no better sensation than feeling like the main engine of your own life. Master of yourself, in love with you.

4. Try to Be a Realist

Three points to reflect on:

a. If you see everything through an "external" perspective, nothing will depend on you. Success will not cause you satisfaction and you will do nothing when faced with failure.
b. If you evaluate all your successes through an "external" lens and failures through an "internal" lens, you will destroy yourself to the point of depression.
c. If you attribute all your success to "internal" factors and failures to "external" ones, you will be fooling yourself. You won't become depressed, but you will be dishonest. This is not a healthy kind of optimism.

Try to operate with an internal locus of control, but as a realist. Be objective with your successes and failures. Take responsibility for what you really had a hand in and not what you wish you had. Points a and b above represent the typical way people with weak self-efficacy think: They are very pessimistic. Point c shows the psychological structure of those who appear to have strong self-efficacy, although it is falsely constructed.

Accept your successes, as it would be unfair not to acknowledge your achievements; but also accept your share of responsibility in your failures. This will allow you to enjoy your victories without guilt or remorse and overcome adversity without false hope. Grab a pen and paper—the written word allows for better analysis—and note your real contribution to the good and bad things that happen to you. Again, just your contribution, ignoring anyone or anything else. Don't be too quick to blame yourself, think about it properly and balance the facts: what you did and what you thought. Congratulate yourself for your achievements and go over your contribution to the failures in order to try to modify them, not to punish yourself. Remember that nothing is ever totally good or bad (get rid of the words "always," "never," "all," or "nothing"). If you only see the unsuitable traits in yourself, your contribution will appear frightful and your self-esteem will be dealt a heavy blow. If you only see the good, you will be a liar living a life clinging to your ego.

5. Don't Only Remember the Bad Things

A negative view of oneself is mainly fed by memories; so if the view you have of yourself is negative, the memories will confirm this blueprint and you will remember more of the bad than the good. If you have weak self-efficacy, your failures will be more readily available in your memory than your successes. Be aware of that and do not get caught up in the cycle of negative memories.

For a few minutes each day, try to activate your positive memory. You will discover the existence of a huge amount of good information about yourself that you had forgotten: positive things you did with your life and with others, acts of bravery, of defense of your rights, of love, of joy. Write down your past successes and try to keep them active and present, without underestimating them or telling yourself "it was nothing." Learn to savor the past and relive its pleasant moments. Nobody wants to see a bad movie on repeat, so don't obsess over the negative. The past is waiting for you to rescue it and to revindicate yourself.

6. Review Your Goals

If your self-efficacy is weak, you will be more likely to err on the side of caution rather than go for broke (as we saw in the self-concept section, when your mind diligently seeks ambition). You will be underestimating yourself and adjusting your goals to the alleged inability you see in yourself. The two extremes are dangerous: If you believe you are invincible, you will tear yourself to shreds; and if you feel incapable, your objectives will be so basic that you will only attempt to take one or two steps. Review your goals and you will see that you can very likely stretch yourself a little more, be more demanding of yourself and be more in line with your true strengths. This does not mean that this will happen immediately. The process of improving self-efficacy takes time. What you need is persistence.

Don't let fear and insecurity make decisions for you. If there are no challenges, resignation will be running your life. Make a list of the things you do not do out of pure fear and ask yourself how many of your dreams and aspirations reflect what you would really like to do and how many have been adapted to your psychological undervaluing of yourself. Ask yourself how much resignation there is in you. Do your current goals show confidence or a lack of confidence in yourself? You have the right to expect more from yourself and from life.

7. Test Yourself and Take a Risk

The previous points are necessary conditions for becoming a person with high self-efficacy, but they are not sufficient. It is vital for you to bring yourself to take the decisive step: taking action to achieve your objectives. And the only way to trust yourself is to put yourself to the test. When you decide to face your fears and insecurities, the previous six steps will help you to not distort reality in favor of your undervaluing of yourself. If you attempt them rationally (without beating yourself up in the process), you will obtain results on your genuine abilities and you will be able to ascertain if the failure predictions you made were true or false. The saying "a bird in the hand is worth two in the bush" will take you nowhere; it is your ticket to conformism and stagnation. What do you have to lose by trying new challenges? Failing once? Don't forget what we mentioned earlier: Nobody learns from trial and success, but through trial and error.

You could propose the following plan to yourself:

- Define an objective that requires effort. The objective should be rational or with a reasonable chance of success. Remember that the "superhero style" also leads to adaptive failure in the real world.
- Define your expectations objectively, clearly, and precisely, so that you can then compare them with the achieved results. When outlining these anticipations, be as sincere as possible. Write them down.
- Before and during the actual execution of the behavior, do not use negative or inhibiting statements; don't say to yourself, "I'm not capable," "Nothing can be done," "I will always be a failure," and so on.
- Use an internal locus of control. Remember those times in your life when you have shown a fighting spirit.
- Test yourself. Without being irresponsible or conducting dangerous behavior, try out what you are afraid of.

- During the showdown, instead of avoiding the obstacles, try to persist for as long as possible. Endure the adrenaline completely; true, it might be uncomfortable, but it is just a chemical that will be absorbed by the organism. Remember, sensations pass and they cannot hurt you.
- Compare the results to the predictions you had written down earlier. Analyze the discrepancies between your predictions and reality; in other words, which predictions came true or not. Try to discover whether your anticipations were guided by fatalism and/or pessimism.
- If so, try again. Ensure that your next attempt at your objective is not steeped in catastrophic predictions. Simply try to be more realistic with your predictions.
- When you feel comfortable and secure with your efforts, move on to a bigger goal. As you increase the level of demands you make of yourself (without causing yourself harm or overexerting yourself), your self-efficacy and self-confidence will increase. You will be able to defeat the Fourth Horseman.

EPILOGUE

If you have come this far, I can only assume that you have properly read the previous pages. It's possible that you have now come to some conclusions about the love you profess for yourself and what to do about it. Perhaps you discovered that you didn't love yourself that much or that you weren't doing it in a convincing way, or you might have reached the conviction that you have always loved yourself enough and these pages have added nothing substantial to what you already knew. This also might have been a good reminder of things that you often forget because you're thinking about others more than yourself. In any case, there are countless roads leading to self-love and you can decide which one to take, which one you like, and which one you don't.

What you should never lose is the ability to seek and question. We often fear creating new goals because they generate new problems and unanswered questions. So we prefer to repress millions of feelings that would bring us closer to new perspectives on life, new sensations, and new discoveries, because it is easier to cling to what we know, even if these things sour our lives. In a certain sense, we are like those stubborn priests who refused to look through Galileo Galilei's telescope in order not to shake their belief that the Earth was the center of the universe—it was easier to suppress genius than to check their beliefs.

If you decide to pull your head out of the sand, there will be uncomfortable moments and upsetting experiences. There will be confusion and doubt. You will discover new contradictions that were not calculated by the traditional education you received, and you will have to become an autodidact (learning by trial and error), simply because we lack clear, transparent rules to help us decipher our inner world. There are no absolute truths, just theories that need to be tested, and what is good for somebody might be bad for somebody else. The initial words of Tagore pinpoint the problem: We struggle between universality (what we share with the entire cosmos) and our small/great individuality, that which makes us different and unique. Perhaps the recent dramatic sociopolitical changes around the world are nothing more than an attempt to recover the forgotten extreme of healthy individualism without losing our sense of belonging to our respective "tribes."

Taking responsibility for yourself is the greatest responsibility. It's understandable that such an undertaking would make us tremble, not just because of the importance it implies, but because we also lack the tools. No national entity has seriously considered the possibility of teaching us to love ourselves as one of the main objectives of education (maybe because we wouldn't be so easily manipulated, and we would escape from the Matrix). Being fully aware of your existence, your importance, and your right to love yourself puts you in a privileged position, but at the same time it produces new anxieties and a great responsibility. Clarity has a price: "I know what I must do, but I don't always know how to do it."

If reading this book has caused some confusion in you, I'm glad. The spirit of important changes lies in underlying doubt and contradiction. A progressive and non-repressive doubt will lead you to review your conceptions, whether to affirm or modify them, and while you go back and forth, you are reaffirming your condition of being alive.

If you were hoping to find definitive categorical truths to give you relief and peace of mind, I'm sorry to disappoint you. Loving yourself, falling in love with your true self, is an arduous task. It implies sailing against the current of sociocultural generalization and intolerance. The following words by Brassens perfectly reflect what I want to express: "It doesn't sit well with people that there is a personal path." THE SOLUTION doesn't exist, it just shifts. Like a pendulum that never stops, we can slow down or speed up its rhythm, but we will never be able to make it stop at an exact point. Guidance on how to strengthen self-love is not always clear, defined, and fixed; however, it is possible to find directives, guidelines, and action plans. Being miserly is damaging to your mental health, so save less. Functioning the whole time with an external locus of control is not ideal, so aim more toward an internal locus of control. Excessive modesty is harmful, so be less modest. In order to love yourself, you should balance the scales in a healthy manner. Basically, I suggest the following: head in the opposite direction of most conventions, without going to the other extreme. That is the challenge: finding your personal space and the suitable distance to love yourself comfortably, without major upheaval or guilt. Despite everything, the mere attempt will be healthy: You will have created the wonderful experience of loving yourself.

BIBLIOGRAPHY

ANDRÉ, C. (2006). *Prácticas de la autoestima*. Buenos Aires: Kairós.

ASSOR, A., VANSTEENKISTE, M., and KAPLAN, A. (2009). Identified versus introjected approach and introjected avoidance motivations in school and in sport: The limited benefits of self-worth strivings. American Psychological Association, 101, 482, 497.

BATTLE, J. (1982). *Enhancing Self-esteem and Achievement: A Handbook for Professionals*. Seattle, WA: Special Child Publication.

BROWN, J. D. and GALLAGHER, F. M. (1992). Coming to terms with failure: private self-enhancement and public self-effacement. *Journal of Experimental Social Psychology*, 28, 3–22.

COMER, J., KENNEDY, S., and LABOUFF, J. (2006). Development and initial validation of implicit measure of humility relative to arrogance. *Journal of Positive Psychology*, 1: 198–211.

DUNKLEY, D. M., ZUROFF, D. C., and BLANKSTEIN, K. R. (2003). Self-critical perfectionism and daily affect: Dispositional and situational influences on stress and coping. *Journal of Personality and Social Psychology,* 84, 234–252.

CHEN, H. and JACKSON, T. (2009). Predictor of change in weight esteem among mainland Chinese adolescents: A longitudinal analysis. *American Psychological Association,* 45, 1618–1629.

CHEN, H. (2010). Significant other and contingencies of self-worth: Activation and consequences of relationship-specific contingencies of self-worth. American Psychology Association, 98, 77–91.

EHRLINGER, J. and DUNNING, D. (2003). How chronic self-views influence (and potentially mislead) estimates of performance. *Journal Personality and Social Psychology,* 84, 5–17.

FERRIS, D. L., BROWN, D. J., LIAN, H., and KEEPING, L. M. (2009). When does self-esteem relate to deviant behavior? The role of contingences of self-worth. American Psychological Association, 94, 1345–1353.

GENTILE, B., GRABE, S., DOLAN-PASCOE, B., and WELLS, B. E. (2009). Gender differences in domain-specific self-esteem a meta-analysis. American Psychological Association, 13, 34–45.

GRANT, H. and DEWECK, C. S. (2003). *Journal of Personality and Social Psychology,* 85, 541–553.

GRZEGOREK, J. L., SLANEY, R. B., FRANZE, S., and RICE, K. G. (2004). Self-criticism, dependency, self-esteem, and grade point average satisfaction among clusters of perfectionists and nonperfectionists. *Journal of Counseling Psychology,* 5, 192–200.

Maddux, J. E. (2002). Self-efficacy. In C. R. Zinder and S. J. López (Comps.), *Handbook of Positive Psychology*. Oxford: University Press.

Meltzer, A. L. and McNulty, J. K. (2010). Body image and marital satisfaction: Evidence for the mediating role of sexual frequency and sexual satisfaction. American Psychology Association, 24, 156–164.

Mruk, C. (1998). *Autoestima. investigación y práctica*. Bilbao: Descleé de Brouwer.

Myers, D. G. (2004). *Exploraciones de la psicología social*. Madrid: Mc Graw-Hill.

Nystul, M. S. and Grade, M. (1979). The self-concept of regular transcendental meditators, dropout meditators and non-meditators. *Journal of Psychology*, 103, 15–18.

Orth, U., Robins, R. W., Trzesniewaki, K. H., Maes, J., and Schmitt, M. (2009). Low self-esteem is a risk factor for depressive symptoms from young adulthood to old age. American Psychology Association, 118, 472–478.

Orth, U., Robins, R. W., and Meier, L. (2009). Disentangling the effects of low self-esteem and stressful events on depression: Findings from three longitudinal studies. *Journal of Personality and Social Psychology*, 97, 307–321.

Orth, U., Trzesniewski, K. H., and Robins, R. W. (2010). Self-esteem development from young adulthood to old age: A cohort-sequential longitudinal study. *Journal of Personality and Social Psychology*, 98, 645–658.

Paradis, A. W. and Kernis, M. H. (2002). Self-esteem and psychological well-being: Implications of fragile self-esteem. *Journal of Social and Clinical Psychological*, 21, 345–361.

Park, C. L., Cohen, L. H., and Myrch, R. (1996). Assessment and prediction of stress-related growth. *Journal of Personality,* 64, 71–105.

Pasini, W. (2001). *L'autoestima.* Milano: Mondadori.

Plummer, J. T. (1985). How personality makes a difference. *Journal of Advertising Research,* 24, 27–31.

Ralph, J. A. and Mekena, S. (1998). Attributional style and self-esteem: The prediction of emotional distress following a midterm exam. *Journal of Abnormal Psychology,* 19898, 203–215.

Rotter, B. (1966). Generalized expectancies for internal versus external control of reinforcement. *Psychological Monographs,* 80 (1), 1–28.

Savater, F. (1988). *Ética como amor propio.* Barcelona: Grijalbo Mondadori.

Seligman, M. E. P. (1981). *Indefensión.* Barcelona: Debate.

Shaffer, D. R. (2000). *Desarrollo social y de la personalidad.* Madrid: Thomson.

Stapel, D. A. and Blanton, H. (2004). From seeing to being: Subliminal social comparisons affect implicit and explicit self-evaluations. *Journal of Personality and Social Psychology,* 87, 468–481.

Tafarodi, R. and Vu, C. (1997). Two-dimensional self-esteem and reactions to success and failure. *Personality and Social Psychology Bulletin,* 23, 626–635.